IT HAD 2 HAPPEN

The Agony of Success

Brian Banks, J.D.

Ms. Gloria,

Thank you for the support + prayers. Much love to you!

Brian

www.TrueVinePublishing.org

It Had 2 Happen: The Agony of Success
By: Brian Banks, J.D.

Copyright © 2020 by Brian Banks

ISBN: 978-1-7357540-3-1 *Paperback*

Editing by : Tiffanie Y. Lewis
Love1Ministries@gmail.com

Cover design by: DeShon Gale & DG Creative Studios

Printed in the United States of America—First Printing

Published by:
True Vine Publishing Co.
P.O. Box 22448
Nashville, TN. 37202
www.TrueVinePublishing.org

For more information about the author or to book for speaking engagements, contact: www.ItHad2Happen.com

DEDICATION

This book is dedicated to several people who played vital roles in my life and meant the world to me.

My Grandfather
April 12, 1929 - April 5, 2011
Dedicated to the memory of my late grandfather, Mr. O.D. Banks. You may be gone but not forgotten. Not a day goes by that I don't think about you and the life lessons you taught me. You were my hero! Thank you for all you did for me but most of all thank you for being present in my life not only as my grandfather but the only father that I really knew!

My Great Aunt
March 30, 1939 - November 8, 2018
Dedicated to the memory of my late great aunt, Alma "Sally" Warren. Thank you for being a safe haven for my mother, Justin, and I. Thank you for exuding love and instilling the importance of family. Thank you for all of the cooking lessons and making sure that I knew how to make everything from dressing to pinto beans, to corned beef & cabbage.

My Friend & Sister
July 18, 1966 – March 29, 2020
Dedicated to the memory of my late friend Rev. Valerie M. Messiah. You were such a great encourager, supporter, and friend. In March of this year, we loss you to COVID-19 but your love and memories will never die. Thank you for your love & friendship and thank you for believing in me and believing that I could solve and handle anything.

ACKNOWLEDGMENTS

I am thankful to God for his unwavering faithfulness and favor towards me. I know without Him I would be nothing.

To my mother, Joyce Banks, I can't even begin to put into words what you mean to me. Thank you for supporting me each and every step of the way. Thank you for living a life of service to your family, friends, and community. Throughout the course of my life you've shown me how to help those who may be in need, even if it's without a thank you.

To my brother, Justin, thank you for being the respectful young man that you are and for allowing me to be more than your older brother, but your protector, advisor, banker, and everything else.

To Joe, thank you for being my best friend and brother. Thank you for your years of support. You've now become a permanent fixture in our family.

To my cousin, Debbie, thank you for being a listening ear down through the years. Thank you for your support, encouragement, and love. Thank you again for answering the calls years ago and coming to my rescue when I was in the middle of my mess!

To my extended family, thank you for your unwavering support, prayers, and encouragement.

To my friends – Ebony Ford, Terrence Tarver, Ron & Angie Kelly, Eric Jackson, Henri Jefferson, Jillian Martin, Esq., Carl Ross, Keith Johnson, Karen Dumas, Donald Trammel, State Representative Sherry Gay-Dagnogo, Pam Martin, State Representative Tenisha Yancey, Esq., LaShantinette Whitaker, Brandi Neal, Elder Robert Moore, Commissioner Jewel Ware, Dr. Iris A. Taylor, Pastor Ronald "Bishop" Alexander, Latisha

Johnson, Kyle Smith, Mildred Gaddis, Mara McDonald, Wayne County Clerk Cathy Garrett, Art Blackwell, Judge E. Lynise Bryant, Judge Regina Thomas, Kristine Longstreet, Esq., Devin Hutchings, Kevin McKinney, Minyon Winfield, Jonathan Davis, Vincent Ingram, Carmen Phillips, Gerald Austin, and Blanche McAllister-Dykes — thank you all for the years of friendship and support. Love you all for life!

To my all star team of volunteers - Deza Sanders, Florea Sutton, Varice Anderson, Wilma Rodgers-Jones, and Margaret Ware — thank you all for always being a part of "Team Bank on Banks".

To my staff and interns — Brian Schmidtke, Esq., Ron Kelly, Rebecca Fadel, J.D., Kyle Giallonardo, J.D., Justin Gardner, and Jazmine Fews. You all held my arms up and kept the office together. Thank you for having a heart to serve the people of the State of Michigan. I am proud of each of your individual successes.

To my mentors – Judge Denise Langford Morris, Retired Judge Vonda Evans, Judge Cylenthia LaToye Miller, and Thomas Stallworth IV – thank you for believing in me. Thank you for your mentorship, wisdom, and counsel down through the years.

Thank you to my pastor, Bishop J. Drew Sheard and First Lady Evangelist Karen Clark-Sheard for your wisdom, support, and teaching.

Thank you, Tiffanie Y. Lewis, for being the much needed book coach and motivator during this process. Your expertise is second to none!

Thank you to my graphic and digital media team, DeShon Gale & DG Creative Studios and Carles Whitlow &

Nine Thirty Marketing. Thank you both for your creative minds and professionalism through this process.

Thank you to each and every supporter down through the years. Whether you've voted for me, gave a campaign contribution, volunteered for an event or Election Day, whispered a prayer or liked a social media post, thank you from the bottom of my heart!

TABLE OF CONTENTS

INTRODUCTION

I believe "going through" in life is all a part of the divine plan. The good, the bad, and the ugly are all part of the process of life. In life there are some things we bring on ourselves while other things come as either a distraction or a lesson to be learned. It's all a part of the plan. Even though I am convinced that there is a winner inside each and every one of us, I have learned that success comes with high moments and low moments. I've also learned that success is not immediate; it takes a process to reach each level of success you will achieve.

You are probably wondering how "agony" and "success" can be in the same sentence. Webster's Dictionary defines "oxymoron" as a "combination of contradictory or incongruous words." In this book, I will take you on my personal journey — the highs, the lows, the good, and the bad. I will be transparent about my path from a law breaker, convicted of multiple felonies, to a law maker as a member of the Michigan State House of Representatives.

I will share intimate details of my life, including my path to living a purposeful life of fulfillment and triumph. I know firsthand what it's like to be underprivileged and disadvantaged because I grew up in a low-income, single-parent household. I am keenly aware of the difficult choices that today's youth face. I, like many people, have dealt with a myriad of decisions and choices in education, careers, family, making ends meet, and more.

It is my hope that, in the event you are introduced to criminal activity, you will learn from my experience and don't have to succumb to that lifestyle. There are more options available to you than breaking the law. As a result of many encoun-

11

ters with the criminal justice system, coupled with having to deal with the effects of the process, I became intrigued to take a further look and start my study of the law. At one point, I lost everything — my car, my apartment, and even some hopes and dreams. I felt hopeless!

It was devastating as I really, and truly, didn't understand how I had allowed myself to get there. I was embarrassed to say the least. Not only was I embarrassed for myself, but I was embarrassed for my family. My poor decisions had altered my life, the reputation of my family and the upward direction I had envisioned for my career aspirations. In my mind, the path was clear: graduate from college, attend law school, graduate again, become a prominent attorney and, then, sit on the bench as an officer of the court. I mean, that's a pretty straight path, right? Wrong!

Every decision that you make will have a lasting effect on you for years to come. Each decision that I made, from roughly 1993 to 2003, impacted me for years. It was like a domino effect. To alleviate a temporary hardship, I sometimes made not-so-smart decisions that had permanent impacts which will follow me the rest of my life. Even a small decision like telling a lie has a lasting effect. You know those *small* lies that we sometimes tell? Many of our decisions, be it big or small, when they are the wrong decisions, can influence our mental and financial health.

When we have to deal with the repercussions of our bad decisions, it weighs on our minds and depression can set in. I had many days when I was depressed. I didn't want to do anything and I didn't want to be around anyone. My finances suffered and, eventually, my employability was ruined. In spite of that, I had no idea that, one day, it was going to work in my favor.

I'm sure, at some point in your life, you have set some personal goals. Most people set goals to be successful and goals to make their families proud. You probably said, "By the time I'm 'this age', I want to have my degree. By the time I'm 'this age', I want to be married or, by the time I'm 'this age', I want to have children." Regardless of what your goal was, you have surely experienced this thing called "life"! Life has a way of coming in and messing up all of your plans. It certainly messed up mine.

Life threw me some curve balls that I wasn't prepared for. I felt like throwing in the towel. Besides the setbacks that I will share with you in this book, I've had countless failures, mind-blowing disappointments, and moments of utter defeat. I have experienced the storms of life. Those storms seemed like every force of opposition was coming against me with all of its might. During this time, I forgot all that I had heard and learned in church, and what I learned from my mother, my grandfather, and others about surviving and making a bad situation good.

Let's be honest, we all have to remember to face our fears and not let a temporary situation be a permanent one. I had to remember that everything I needed to succeed was already inside of me. My hope is that through my story, you will grab hold to your faith, breathe, take one day at a time, set some goals, put a plan in place, use some discipline, and execute that plan.

Everything you need is already in you. You're already successful. The mere fact that you're breathing and reading this book tells me that you're a winner. You already have the necessary mental and physical stamina along with the ability to withstand any hardship, setback, or disappointment. There is greatness inside of you. You just have to pull it out!

One thing that helped me get through my many hardships and defeats was my faith in God, coupled with, a great support system with my mother, grandfather, and many others. I had to remember things that my grandfather often said to me like, "Anything worth having, is worth working for" and "Rome wasn't built overnight." Please understand that dreams and goals take hard work and time to realize. So, if you are the one who got in trouble with the law — stay strong and keep going. If you are the one who had a baby at a young age — life's not over. If you are the one who got divorced — you can always begin again. Confront your issues and become the champion of them.

It is my desire that sharing my journey will show you how to get back on track when you do lose your focus and all hope. I will show you that it's possible to still achieve those goals even after the storms of life. I pray that my story encourages and inspires you, but also that it causes you to think about your life from the perspective that, on your journey to success, you will have some bumps in the road. It won't always be easy, but they are necessary to get you to your final destination. I want you to see that it's possible to go through it and overcome any obstacles. Trouble won't last always and the sun can shine again in your life.

It took me a long time to embrace my journey because I was ashamed. When I finally embraced it, things started to fall in line. So, don't run from your story, pain or struggle, instead embrace it. It's all going to make sense in the end.

My struggle and pain helped to change the trajectory of my thinking and the core of my character. I no longer looked at setbacks as bad, but as an opportunity to reset, regroup, and learn the lesson from the setback. I had to stop seeing the glass as half empty, but instead as half full. My total perspective had to change.

There were times when everything that could go wrong went wrong and I had to learn to make lemonade out of lemons. When life has kicked you down and you're lying on your back, there's only one way to go and that's up. I had to learn, and you will too, that with strong determination, your agony, despite any failure, can lead to success beyond your wildest imagination!

A BLENDED FAMILY

I was a shy and quiet little boy. I used to sit and observe what was going on around me without saying anything. Slowly, but surely, I started posing more and more questions about the things that I saw. Before I knew it, I became an inquisitive, daring, adventurous, risk-taking and rebellious teenager. By the time I was an adult, though, I was pensive, reflective, analytical and quite the perceptive man. But let me tell you about the beginning.

My grandfather, O.D., was born in North Little Rock, Arkansas, and was the eldest of ten children. My grandmother, Mary, and my grandfather, O.D., were married when they were teenagers. Together, they had two children, my uncle, Alvin, and my mother, Joyce. At a young age, my grandfather dropped out of school to get a job to help take care of his family. After several years of marriage, my grandparents divorced and my grandmother, Mary, moved to New Jersey with her mother, my great grandmother. Both my mother and my uncle stayed in Detroit with my grandfather and his parents. My grandfather raised my mom and my uncle with the help of my great grandparents.

When my uncle Alvin graduated from high school and became an adult, he moved away and began living his life and started his own family. I was raised by my mother and her father. I didn't know who my father was for a long time. My grandfather didn't have another son beside Alvin. Since I lived with him, my grandfather treated me as if I was his son rather than his grandson.

16

My grandfather was a proud man who had an exemplary work ethic. He worked for General Motors for over twenty-five years and never missed a day. O.D. Banks was my everything! He was my banker, my friend, my supporter and my disciplinarian. Now, I must honestly also tell you that my grandfather was quite bossy. He had many phrases that he would say regularly such as, "It costs to be the boss" or "Do as I say, not as I do."

My grandfather was not one to "spare the rod", and often disciplined me and my cousins, when necessary. When he would discipline us, he would often say, "It hurts me more to do this than it's going to hurt you." He was a no-nonsense guy. I learned a lot of life lessons from my grandfather. I even got my sense of style from him and he really took pride in his appearance. When my grandfather put on his dress clothes, you couldn't tell him that he wasn't sharp!

One of the many things I admired about my grandfather was that, despite his shortcomings, he had a relationship with God. Not a day went by that I didn't hear my grandfather downstairs in the basement praying for his family. One time I tipped downstairs to see what he was doing, and to my surprise, he was on his knees, in front of the sofa, praying. This did my heart good as my family established a foundation of prayer and faith in me at an early age.

Even when my grandfather was mad or disappointed with one of his family members, he never let it stand in the way of him "being the man" and providing for his family. My grandfather taught me that family was supposed to stick together. He had a very close bond with his brothers and sisters. Being the eldest of them all, my grandfather thought he could boss his siblings around, even with them being married with children. Despite my maternal grandparents divorcing at an early age, they remained friends. My grandfather would drive my mother and me to New Jersey to spend time with my grandmother and our other family members. This was before my brother, Justin, was born. My grandmother would come back to Detroit to visit and would come by my grandfather's house to see everyone. We seemed like a pleasant family, but we had issues at my grandfather's house.

I like to think of my immediate family as me, my mother, my brother, Justin, and my grandfather. Unfortunately, the three of us did not live in O.D. Banks' house alone. Sometime in the sixties, my grandfather met a lady named Rose and they eventually moved in together. My grandfather and Rose had two children together, Jackie and Kim. Michigan had something called a "common law marriage" that allowed people who lived together for 10 years or more to be considered legally married. They were together for at least 20 years before I believe they legitimately got married around 1979.

This lady was unlike anyone I had ever met. I often wondered why my grandfather had married Rose. What did he see in her? She was demeaning and nasty to his children and family. I couldn't quite understand how a woman (Rose) could be married to a man (O.D.) and not accept the man's children and grandchildren from his first marriage. *What adult would teach and instill jealousy, hate and envy in their children?* There was always an issue in our household and unfortunately most issues revolved around O.D.'s relationships with his other children and grandchildren. *Why would he subject our family to this?*

My grandfather had a female friend who was actually a longtime friend of the Banks family named Alice. Ms. Alice and her family treated my mother, Justin and me so much better than Rose, Kim, and Jackie treated us. Ms. Alice and her family welcomed us just like we were a part of their family. There were never any issues, arguments, or disagreements. Ms. Alice would often let me use her car and, when I first got my driver's license, I would often take her to doctor's appointments and to the grocery store. *Why couldn't he have married her?*

The older I became, the more I realized that my step-family was quite jealous of the relationship that my grandfather had with us. My grandfather and I had a special bond. He treated me as if I was his son rather than his grandson. Even though I didn't know my biological father, my grandfather made sure I lacked nothing. I loved spending time with my grandfather. Every week he took me to the credit union with him while he transacted his banking. I tagged along with my grandfather everywhere. He was a provider who believed in "quasi" tough love. Even with that, my bond with my grandfather was unbreakable.

My grandfather did his best to take good care of all of his children and family and he did a great job, might I add. Even with a limited education, he provided and made sure that no one went without. My grandfather made sure that Kim had a new car every couple of years, and even though they were in Rose's name, my grandfather paid the car insurance for all of her vehicles and helped Rose with the car payments. My grandfather bought and assisted my Uncle Alvin with the purchase of several vehicles and often times loaned him money that was not repaid. Although Jackie was married and had a family of her own, my grandfather always made sure Jackie was taken care of. He even assisted her with getting a divorce attorney when she and her husband were getting a divorce.

My grandfather also had another daughter, Tonesa, who we called "Toni", who didn't come around often as she lived with her mom. Aunt Toni and I began to get close as we both worked at the same job for a while and also had a lot of things in common. I really looked up to Aunt Toni because she knew how to dress (I thought I could dress a little bit) and she seemed to have her life together. I enjoyed talking with her and I enjoyed being around her the few times that she came around. She wasn't like my other two step-aunts, Kim and Jackie.

Toni had experienced some of the same things that my mother and I experienced from Rose, Kim and Jackie. You know, being intertwined with a blended family and all. She and I both had our stories as it relates to family and family hurts. When my Aunt Toni went to purchase a new house, she needed a cosigner and my grandfather gladly cosigned for her. My grandfather took me along with him and Toni to the closing for the house. He was just that kind of man.

Many years later, my Step-aunt Toni got into some trouble with her then boyfriend, "T." When the indictment came down and my aunt was arrested, I was totally shocked as the media was betraying them like the mob. The news media was reporting that this was one of the largest indictments ever. *Hold up, my aunt was a part of the internationally known group called "Black Mafia Family" better known as "BMF"?* Toni shared with my grandfather some of the details of what was going on with her, but she didn't want him to worry. As a result, she kept some things from him.

After going through her court proceedings, eventually, Toni ended up having to go to prison for a couple of years. I, along with many other family members and friends, accompanied Toni to court on her sentencing day. She was later housed at a correctional facility in California. She would often call and speak with my grandfather, but would keep it short so he didn't ask any questions. Toni and I frequently emailed each other and I flew out there one time to see and check on her. To this day, Toni and I remain close.

My mother was very quiet and, most of the time, she kept to herself. My mother was this small, petite lady, who loved to be on the go. She loved shopping and traveling. As a child, it grieved me seeing was how she was treated "less than" by Rose and her stepsisters. I often would watch how they dealt with my mother and how they expected her to behave. It was my own version of *Cinderella* and her wicked stepsisters, except for my mother's father was still there!

My grandmother Mary's husband, Slim, never treated us like Rose handled us. This will always be a mystery to me. Rose, Kim, and Jackie would talk to my mother any kind of way, say mean things behind her back, and would expect her to be the cleanup lady. My mother is extremely giving and still, to this day, will give anyone the shirt off of her back. This is where I get my giving and serving characteristics from.

Even with how we were treated, my mother, brother and I regarded Rose as our own blood up until her death. My grandfather loved all of his family (wife, children and grandchildren) and made sure we all were provided for in some way or another. He did not make a difference between children and grandchildren. My grandfather wanted everyone to get along. Unfortunately, that only lasted for a little while.

When my brother, Justin, was born, I did not want him to experience some of the things that I saw and experienced. Justin and I are night and day. While we physically favor, I talk a lot and Justin doesn't. I will call you out and check you, but

Justin will ignore you unless you really push him to respond. There is a little more than a thirteen-year difference in age between Justin and me. He eventually saw the mistreatment that we received and, when he became older, he often questioned it, too.

I don't know about you, but when I think of a rose, I think of a beautiful, delicate, sweet-smelling flower. Roses represent positive emotions and feelings shared between people for special occasions. The colors of roses are known to represent love (red), purity (white) and even friendship (yellow). Of course, roses do have their thorns, which are known to protect them from plant-eating species. However, the Rose I grew up with had no soft petals. She was all thorns and she used them to attack me and my family on a regular basis.

What's This Lady's Problem?

A typical day at our house consisted of my step-grandmother, Rose, drinking two to three 40-ounces after she came home from work. She had an argument with either my grandfather or my mother every day. I thought to myself, "What's this lady's problem? Does she not like us? Does she not want us here?" After a series of outlandish events, I realized that I was right. She really didn't want us there and it wasn't just her that didn't care for us.

Her daughter, Jackie, would come over to our house every day. Jackie would cook her family's food and wash their clothes at our house. I often wondered, "Why won't she go home? Do they not have lights and gas?" Jackie's husband, Clarence, was an architectural engineer. They lived in a historic home in Indian Village and they appeared to be the perfect family, but they were just always at our house.

I didn't pay attention to it then, but when I spent the night over there, I remember making palettes and sleeping in front of the fireplace instead of in the bedroom. I overheard my Uncle Clarence complaining that the heat bill was $900 a month. I suppose that's why they came to our house so much — for heat!

Rose would sometimes cook dinner for my grandfather, herself, Kim, my mother, my brother, me, my aunt, Jackie, Clarence, and their two children, Anthony and Jennifer. She was cooking dinner for ten people, but she would only have one chicken and a few extra pieces. It was like four legs, four wings, four thighs, two breasts — no more, no less. The macaroni and cheese was often served in a small Pyrex dish. Most of the time, there was not enough to go back for seconds. *Were we poor?*

We lived in a three-bedroom duplex home on the eastside of Detroit. When it came to dinner, it seemed as if we ate in shifts because there would be more people at the house than the folks who actually lived there. My grandfather, my mother, my brother, and I would eat and then Rose and her family would eat. It was like two separate families in one house. Somehow, I didn't think food was scarce because we didn't have the money. My grandfather worked at General Motors for twenty-five years. He boasted that he went to work every day and he took good care of his family, but that's just how we lived. So, what was it?

I had so many questions racing in my mind on a constant basis. *What kind of environment is this for anyone to live in?* The constant arguing, conditional love, and lack of affection just felt unbearable. *Why would my grandfather make us stay here? Why would he make us live in this environment where my mom always has to argue and fight?* There was verbal, mental, and emotional abuse on a daily basis. There were disagreements every, single day about nothing and something at the same time. If Cinderella were a boy, his name would have been *Brian!*

I remember when my step-aunt, Jackie, was getting married. Everyone was in the wedding except me. My aunts, my uncle, my grandfather, my mom, my cousins — they were all a part of the wedding party. The wedding was at our family's church, which was a huge, Baptist church on the eastside of Detroit. Mt. Calvary had about 2,000 members and a very affluent congregation at that time. My great, great uncle officiated the wedding.

After the wedding, when the wedding party was taking pictures, everybody was assembling themselves to get into the picture. My grandfather pulled me up into one of the pictures and all of a sudden, there was a big commotion. They didn't want me in the pictures! Yeah, I did have on a navy-blue suit and everyone else had on peach and cream, but I felt like it shouldn't have been a problem for me to be in maybe just one of the pictures. Just one! I didn't know what that was about, but it was very hurtful. In fact, a couple of years later, we were looking at the pictures and my cousin, Anthony, said, "Well, we can just have you removed out of the picture profession-ally." Who says that?

There were so many instances when I felt like I wasn't wanted and I couldn't understand why it had to be this way. I kept thinking, "My mother and Uncle Alvin existed before my step-grandmother and grandfather were married. So, if you take the man you got to take his children as well." However, I often watched my mother cry and wished that she didn't have to live with her father and our stepfamily. I didn't understand why my grandfather was making us stay here and for years I carried a lot of resentment toward him.

On one occasion, I remember when I overheard Rose and Jackie downstairs in the kitchen talking about me, my mother, and several other family members. I was upstairs in my room, watching TV and simultaneously doing some homework. I was in such disbelief that adults would say some of the things that they were saying that I decided to grab my mini recorder. I was going to record what they were saying so I could share with my other family members.

Rose said to Jackie, "I don't want them here and I don't know why O.D. has them here." Rose went on to say some mean things about my grandfather and his brothers, my great uncles. I knew that wasn't going to sit well with my great aunts, Sally and Gloria Lee. Jackie would chime in from time to time with her comments and support Rose in her derogatory statements. While they were talking, I could also hear Rose pouring and sipping on one of her 40-ounces.

They would never repeat some of the things they said to my grandfather's face or any other family members for that matter. I couldn't understand for the life of me how people who were supposed to be "family" could say the most hurtful and hateful things about other family members. It was quite perplexing to see and live in an environment that was so different from the definition of family that my grandfather gave and lived.

One thing I knew for sure was that Rose, Jackie, and Kim were jealous of the relationship that my mother and I had with my grandfather. They did not like the closeness we had or the things that my grandfather did for us. They acted as if my grandfather shouldn't take care of his first-born daughter. I guess my grandfather knew, deep down within, who would be there for him in his time of need and that was my mother, my brother, Justin, and me. He never made us feel bad for being there. By the same token, there were times I felt like he could have corrected some of this.

Christmas time was the worst! As a kid you just looked for gifts and for there to be love and affection. Most of the time, the only gifts under the tree for me were from my mother and my grandfather. There was nothing from Rose, Jackie, Kim, Clarence, or any of my so-called "cousins", despite the fact that my mother and I would buy gifts for everyone!

One year my grandfather asked me and my cousin, Anthony, what we wanted for Christmas. When we told him what we wanted, he said, "Well, I'm not going to go to the store to get it, but I'll give you the money to get it." Then, he would put some money in an envelope and, before Christmas Day, he gave us those envelopes so we could go get all of the things we wanted for Christmas. That would have been great every year, but we lived in a house with Rose, Kim and Jackie (she was always there, so you may as well say she lived there).

They bought my cousins gifts, but they never bought me anything. This was extremely troubling for me as I respected Rose, as my elder and as my grandfather's wife, and I treated her like my biological grandmother and not a step-grandmother. *Why won't she treat me the same as her other grandchildren?*

Rose, who I was supposed to respect and obey, is the same woman who was spiteful and who intentionally said things that were insensitive and malicious to a child. The conversation in my mind about why we were in the same house with her seemed hopeless and endless. I thought God had something to do with it, too. I asked Him questions, too. *God, are you punishing me? I'm living in a house where I'm not wanted and my mom is not wanted.* I didn't get the answers I was looking for, and many nights, lying in the bed, I just cried. I said to myself, "You know, I have to be the man. I've got to get a job. I want to take care of my mother. I want to get us out of this house."

On many nights, I was often awake because my grandfather and step-grandmother would argue all night and I would not get much sleep. I would get to school and I would be sleepy, tired, and on top of that, I wasn't being challenged in class. So, I began to go to school and skip class, which really didn't make much sense. I loved school!

In school, I was a very talkative child, but I did my work. I enjoyed English. I enjoyed writing. I enjoyed music. I was always interested in school especially during my elementary school years. I was excited about school and I earned very good grades. Early in my middle school days, my mother and I discovered that I wasn't being challenged in school. I would often times get done with my work before my classmates, as the work seemed to be too easy. Many days I would finish my class work and sit at my desk and think about my home life. I would think about my living arrangements and how it seemed so unfair. Despite dealing with family problems and an unpleasant home life, I still managed to keep my grades up.

During my eighth-grade year, I learned about University Liggett, a very prestigious school in Grosse Pointe Woods. I spoke to my teacher, Mrs. Brantley, who told me it would be a good opportunity for me. She agreed to set up a day for me to visit the school. I received permission from Mrs. Brantley and my mother to miss a whole day of class to go tour the new school. I didn't even have a way to get to the school, but my next-door neighbor, Earl, was a taxi cab driver and he was able to take me to visit the new school.

At University Liggett I had the opportunity to meet some students that went to the school who were my age and in the same grade. At first, it was very intimidating because the school reminded me of a college campus. The lawn was well manicured, the roses on the rose bushes had started to bloom, and there was no litter on the grounds. I thought to myself, "This can't be a middle school." The students were all well-mannered and respectful. This was not what I was accustomed to at my school. Every day I saw fights among students, class-room disruptions, and even saw students getting into physical altercations with the teachers and staff.

During my visit, I was paired with a student named Jeremy. Jeremy and I discussed the different things we were doing in school and the lessons we were learning and how those lessons were being taught. It just seemed like they were receiving so much more! The classroom sizes were smaller with 12-15 students in each class compared to our 30. The students were excelling greatly compared to my school where the students were just marginally making it. The teachers at University Liggett seemed to make learning fun. They engaged each student and made sure that everyone understood the lesson.

We also talked about our families. Jeremy's father was an executive at Chrysler and his mother was a registered nurse. Jeremy was one of about 10-15 African Americans at the school. At lunch time there was a smorgasbord of options to eat. In the late Eighties this school had a salad bar and a shake machine! We weren't in a lunch room. We were in a cafeteria. There wasn't any of the fighting, arguing, or the food throwing going on that I was accustomed to. Students were studying and eating.

I recall sitting in a math class with Jeremy and I was lost. It was the eighth grade, but I was surprised to see how the students were engaged in the learning process. It was a culture shock. I didn't have to worry about the teacher constantly stopping to deal with disciplinary issues or classroom management issues. I don't remember what the exact mathematic subject was, but I recall thinking, "We're not supposed to learn that until 11th or 12th grade!" They seemed so much more advanced than we were at my school.

The whole environment was just conducive for learning. I didn't hear a lot of noise. I could feel students learning. I saw students actively participating and being engaged in the learning process. They were asking questions, giving feedback to the teachers, and they were genuinely excited to learn. This was so different from my school, but this was something that I desired because I loved school at that time. I was especially enthused to learn that most students who graduate from University Liggett would go on to college. I was motivated, inspired, and energized to try and get there. Who would have thought that an eighth grader from the Harper and Dickerson area on the east side of Detroit would have an opportunity to go to a prestigious school such as University Liggett?

Needless to say, I became quite interested in attending that school. I came home after the tour exhilarated, but the school came with a big price. Tuition for an eighth grader was around fifteen to twenty-thousand dollars per year. I knew my family didn't have it, but the good thing was that they had a scholarship for a certain number of disadvantaged students. I brought the documents home anyway and sat at the kitchen table to discuss it with my mother. We were going over the application and preparing to complete it. It asked a lot of questions, especially about my mother's financial information.

Then Rose, who was in the kitchen, drinking and cooking, just decided she had to interrupt our conversation. "You need to keep yo' ass right there in that public school and keep yo' ass where you know the people. You don't need to go to that school. Y'all don't know anything about that school. You just need to hope that you get out of school and finish school!"

She continued with a whole lot of other negative comments. I was in total shock and disbelief. *How could someone speak like this to me, especially when I want to do something better for myself?* I was extremely disappointed that I didn't have the full support of my family.

Rose seemed offended by the fact that I had gone to the school and I was inside it and I really wanted to pursue it. It was as if she thought I really didn't belong there. She made me feel like I wasn't good enough for it. Looking back on it, she probably just had some personal jealousy and insecurity issues. My mother stopped and told Rose that what she was saying was wrong and she was out of line. "If that's where I want him to go, that's where he's going to go, especially if it's a better opportunity for him!" my mother quipped.

My mother is, and always has been, a quiet, soft-spoken woman who unselfishly gives of herself. My mother worked for many years in the healthcare industry and several nursing homes and hospitals. My mother's passion is caring for others. However, this particular day, my mother and I had had enough of Rose. There were many arguments and fights in that house, but I was determined that this was going to be the last one!

Rose began to belittle and berate my mother and that was it. When Rose started approaching my mother in an aggressive manner, I jumped in to protect my mother and that's when it went down. When Rose went to swing at my mother, we fought Rose's drunk ass from the kitchen, to the living room and to the bathroom. Before it was over, a ceramic garbage can ended up being broken over Rose's head!

When my grandfather came home, my mother and I were sitting in the living room and Rose had fallen asleep in the bedroom in a drunken stupor. He could look at our faces and tell something was wrong. He looked around the house and observed the furniture in disarray. Then, he looked at the broken garbage can. "What happened here?" he asked. "Ask your wife," my mother grimaced, "because I've had enough of her!"

My grandfather went in the bedroom to question her and he discovered that she was still inebriated. The two of them got into a very heated argument. He knew he didn't have to ask any more questions because of the state she was in. He knew what had happened. He knew it was all her fault.

I'll never forget that night. It changed my life forever. My grandfather picked the phone up and called his sister, Sally, and told her he was bringing my mother and me over to her house to stay the night. My grandfather told me and my mother to get some of our things and that he was taking us to Aunt Sally's house. I preferred to be there anyway. It was much more like a family. Everyone treated everyone like family there. My aunt cooked plenty of food, and I didn't feel like I didn't belong.

Over the next couple of days, I started thinking that maybe I shouldn't try to pursue better. After all, my grandfather worked at General Motors as an hi-low driver. Rose was a housekeeper at St. John Hospital. It wasn't like they had white collar jobs. Who was I to even want better? Who was I to even dream of better? I ended up not even applying to University Liggett. The next day I returned to my school and Mrs. Brantley had a lot of questions about how it was to visit the school and what the difference was between there and my school. She was very encouraging and she just thought it was a good opportunity for me. She saw something in me. She knew what I was capable of and she saw that I wasn't maximizing my potential.

After a couple days, I went back to my grandfather's house. My mother remained at my great aunt's house a little while longer. My grandfather came and got me and had a talk with me on our drive home. He shared with me his plans to get us our own place to live. He told me about his conversations with Rose and his disappointment with her. My mother came back home soon after me. Things started off okay, but it wasn't too long before, the insults and arguments began again as a result of Rose's drinking. I finally graduated from the eighth grade and was entering the world of high school.

What's really interesting is that even when I was mad at how Rose treated me, I didn't stay mad for long. When I became an adult, I can remember several occasions when I came into some big money, from either a bonus from a job, my income tax return, or taking a chance at my luck, I would often go to my grandfather's house to share with him what I had. However, I didn't just share with my grandfather, I would share with Rose as well. If I gave my grandfather five hundred dollars, I would give Rose two hundred dollars.

My grandfather was there for me since the day I was born. He never left my side. My grandfather showed me what a true family bond was. You know it is real when you can't walk away from someone. No matter what I did, he was always there. Even though my biological father wasn't in my life, I'm not sure I got a raw deal without a father at all because my grandfather was present and involved. In fact, I think for me, it went the very best way it could have. All the same, I often wonder what my life would have been like if my biological father was involved and engaged in my life.

WHO'S MY DADDY?

As a child, my life wasn't perfect, yet it was better than others. I loved school, I loved church, and I loved my family, but there was something (or should I say someone) missing. My childhood had many family hurts, pains, and disappointments. One of the greatest disappointments sitting with me was that I didn't know who my father was. All of the other kids around me either had both of their parents at home with them or at least knew who both of their parents were and had some form of relationship with them. At that time, I wouldn't know my father if he walked up beside me on the street. I couldn't even identify him in a lineup. As a child that was a difficult pill for me to swallow.

Now, don't get me wrong, in the absence of my father, my grandfather, O.D., stepped up to the plate and was my father and grandfather. However, I believe fathers give sons their identity. This was one area that I felt like I was being short changed. My cousins and friends had both of their parents and I did not. This really weighed on me heavily for years. However, my grandfather did the best he could to be there for me, for which I'm appreciative, and I thank God for him being in my life. Nonetheless, it was still a difficult time for me not knowing who my father was and not knowing my father's side of the family.

Having dropped out of high school, several family members felt I was going to go down the wrong path and I ultimately became the black sheep of the family. Rose, Kim and Jackie were in my grandfather's ear saying I would never be anything and that he needed to wash his hands of me. Well, I knew that that was not going to happen. I just needed a way out.

Yes, I had dropped out of school and it probably wasn't the wisest thing to have done, but I knew that wasn't going to be my end. I knew, somehow or someway, I was going to turn my whole situation around. I was confident that my story was going to end better than what others predicted. It was extremely hurtful to hear so-called "family members" say, "You know, you'll never be anything." At times, I daydreamed about the true meaning and true example of family and of love. It seemed that I frequently had thoughts about how things would be if my father was in my life.

One thing that I loved to do, and it would relieve my mind of a lot, was going to church. I was very active in our church and had many friends there. Most Sundays my grandfather would take my mother and me to church. When he had to work on Sundays, we would have the church van to come and pick us up. Our Sundays typically started with Sunday School, which meant we would have to be up and ready bright and early for the van.

Every Sunday there was a girl named Felicia on the van with us. Felicia was always with one of her friends. Over the years Felicia and I became cool. One Sunday we had an afternoon service and a guest church was invited to our service. Everyone who rode the church van that Sunday decided that we were going to stay for the afternoon service and eat dinner at church in between services.

After the choir sang, our choir members retreated to the congregation to allow the guest choir to take the choir stand. While the guest preacher was up, many of us young folks became a little distracted as we were passing notes and looking at graduation pictures. While I was going through Felicia's graduation pictures, I saw a pocket sized birth certificate and the name listed as father was "Marvin Stokes." I said to Felicia, "Wow, my father's name is Marvin Stokes." We paid it no mind and continued talking and passing notes during church service. A few weeks later, one of our church members said to Felicia and me, "Boy, do the two of you look alike. Has anyone ever told you two that?" We both were shocked as no one had told us that previously, but we didn't really pay it any attention and continued doing what we were doing.

As the months went by, Felicia and I didn't think much about people's comments about us looking alike, but it began to come up more frequently. One day, a church mother asked if we were brother and sister and we replied, "No, but several people say we look alike." I obliviously added, "Our fathers have the same name, too." The church mother was confused by my statement. We had to share with her how we found out that our fathers had the same name.

At that point, Felicia asked me, "How does your father look?" I honestly couldn't answer that as I hadn't seen him since I was five or six years old. My mother had to work that Sunday and was not at church, so Felicia and I went to the church phone and called my mother to ask her to describe my father's appearance. My mother described my father to Felicia and Felicia said, "You just described my father!" Felicia said when she got home, she was going to tell her mother as well.

Later that evening Felicia called me to tell me that she told her mother and her mother asked her father if he had a son named Brian. Felicia said he paused and said, "Yes, how do you know?" They shared that Felicia and I had gone to church together for years and just recently decided to look into it as several people had told us we looked alike. It turned out that he wasn't just Felicia's father, he was my father, too. But unlike Felicia, I didn't know him. I knew nothing about him.

My father went on to share with my sister, Felicia, and her mother that my mother would not allow him to see me, which I knew, and later confirmed, to not be true. I got my father's telephone number from Felicia and planned to call him the next day. Talk about strange! It was weird. I was about to call a man that I didn't know. *What was I going to say? How was the conversation going to go?*

As I prepared to make the call, I didn't know what to say. Would "Hey Dad" work or "May I speak with Marvin" or what? I went with "Is this Marvin?" Hell, I was sixteen years old and had NO relationship with him. The call was very dry and awkward. My father told me that I had some other siblings including Delano, Marvin Jr., Jamar, and that he may have another one or two. I guess you can say, "Papa was a rolling stone!" He invited me to come and visit him so I took his address down and told him that I would have one of my friends bring me over there on the weekend.

When Saturday came it was time for me to go visit my father. He actually lived really close to us. Again, those thoughts began to go through my mind. *How is this going to go?* When I arrived at my father's house, I told my friend to wait outside and that I would not be long. I walked up and knocked on the door. I could hear the television and the voices of two people talking inside. Moments later, the door opened and there was a man standing there that I looked just like. I couldn't believe it. I was looking at an older version of me.

He invited me in. There was another man inside who he introduced as one of his friends. They were both drinking beer and watching TV. I could tell by their slurred speech that they both had probably had a little too much to drink. *I really won't be here long.* My father's friend kept saying, "Yup Marvin, that's yo' child. He looks just like you." My father was appearing somewhat embarrassed. He said ,"Yes, that's my son and I haven't seen him in years."

As I sat there, I couldn't help but wonder why my father had not come to find me? After all, my Aunt Sally still lived in the same house that my great grandparents lived in. Other relatives had lived in the same house for years. He made no effort. I finally asked him why he hadn't tried to find me and his response was deplorable. His response and excuse didn't make any sense to me. I sat in disbelief as I thought, "How could a man abandon his own child?"

My father and his friend continued drinking as we were talking and at one point, they began to argue with each other. My father asked me a question and when I replied, "Oh ok, yeah," he raised his voice sternly saying, "Don't say 'yeah' to me! You need to say 'yes sir, no sir' to me." I looked around as if to say, "I know he's not talking to me." It was pretty clear that he didn't know me and how quick I was with my tongue.

I quickly told him, "The lady who has been both my mother and father don't require me to say 'yes ma'am, no ma'am' to her and the man that has filled in your shoes, my grandfather, don't require me to say 'yes sir, no sir' to him so I will not say it to you! You have never even purchased diapers for me so it's a privilege that I'm here now talking to you!" After all, he lived with Felicia and my brother, Delano, and their mom. They benefitted from his Chrysler checks, not me.

He was quite shocked at my retort, to say the least, and continued to raise his voice and use profanity. His friend began to tell him that he was wrong and needed to stop, but he didn't. I looked at him and said, "I came and met you and shouldn't have." I told his friend that it was nice to meet him and abruptly left.

When I got in my friend's car and told him what happened, my friend was flabbergasted. We arrived back to my house and I saw my grandfather sitting outside on the porch. When I told my mother and grandfather how things went, my grandfather said, "You shouldn't have gone. At this point, you don't need him." My mother said, "I see he hasn't changed a bit." My mother did say something like, "You didn't have to be disrespectful to him." I quickly retorted that respect was earned and not given and he had not earned my respect. As far as I was concerned, he had a lot of making up to do.

A few weeks later, Felicia called me and said she heard what happened and we needed to work things out. She said she understood how I felt, but he was still my father. I told her she was exactly correct he was my father, but had been missing in action for seventeen years. I went on to tell her that she and Delano had the advantage, if nothing else, of knowing who their father was and having a relationship with him. I told her that I would give some thought of trying again with our father.

After a couple weeks went by, I decided to go see him again. By this time, he had moved to a duplex off of Gratiot and East McNichols. I was also driving and had my own car (a 1995 Mustang). I decided that I would take my brother, Justin, with me as we had somewhere else to go afterwards. When I pulled up outside my father's house, there was a guy and girl sitting on the porch. The guy favored me. As I walked up on the porch and spoke, the guy said, "You're Brian?" I replied, "Yes." He told me that he was my brother, Delano.

39

Justin and I went inside quickly so we could leave quickly. My father was sitting at the table eating some fried chicken. I introduced him to Justin and told him we were just stopping by to see how he was doing. There wasn't much noteworthy conversation, but one thing was a repeat from my first visit – he was drunk!

After being there roughly fifteen minutes, I could tell that the conversation was about to take a left turn and possibly a repeat from our first meeting. I stood up to get ready to leave and then it started. My father started cussing and asking where I was going. I knew then we weren't going to get along. I told him I had to go and grabbed Justin and we left.

I later discovered that there were some concerns from several family members about me and when my mother conceived me. Clearly, my father had not been honest with neither my mother nor Felicia and Delano's mother. He was still married to her when I was born. Not to mention that my brother Delano and I were close in age. *Hell, take that issue up with Marvin Stokes, not me and my mother.* I often wondered what my other two brothers, Marvin Jr. and Jamar, were like. Felicia disclosed that Marvin was incarcerated and no one had met Jamar.

I asked for Marvin's contact information and sent him a letter in prison. We began to write each other and he called occasionally. *Wow, I have other brothers and I haven't even met them!* This was exciting, but strange at the same time. Marvin and I lost contact, but eventually reconnected and met in person when he was released. When he came home, he became a barber and established a nice clientele at his barber shop. I would occasionally go and let him cut my hair so we can chat and catch up on things. This is still a norm for us even today.

Months went by and I had not reached out to my father nor had he reached out to me. I spoke with Felicia periodically and she would give me updates on our father. By this time, my father was living with Felicia, so I decided to go by Felicia's house to see him. I waited a couple days and ended up going to Felicia's house the day before Thanksgiving.

When I arrived to Felicia's house, my father was in the bathroom grooming himself. When he was done, he came in the living room where I was and sat across from me. He inquired how my mother and I were doing. I told him we both were good. I asked him how he had been and he shared that he had been diagnosed with cancer. I was shocked and really didn't know what to say. My faith kicked in and I shared with him that God was still a healer and that he had to trust and believe God to heal him. He acknowledged what I said and replied, "I know." He told me that he had lost my telephone number and to put my telephone number in his telephone book. This time we spoke for over an hour. This conversation was much better as there was no profanity and loud talking.

As I began to think about it, I felt strange. I really did not know this man. *Was it too late to get to know him?* He clearly didn't seem to know how to build a relationship with me. One thing was certain, I knew that I was not going to get along with him and his drinking as I was already dealing with one of those problems at home. I didn't want to share with my grandfather how I really felt because I knew he was going to have a lot to say. I often wondered if my grandfather felt slighted in any kind of way because I wanted to know who my biological father was. After all, my grandfather had held all of the duties of a father down.

41

Time went by and things were back to how they had been. I hadn't heard from my father and the number I had was no longer in service. I occasionally would ask Felicia how he was doing and she would share with me. Several times Felicia shared that she and my father was bumping heads while he lived in her house. "Oh, so it wasn't just me?" I thought to myself. I was shocked to hear Felicia and my father were having disagreements. Felicia shared that our father was bull headed and wanted everything to go his way. That didn't surprise me one bit.

Years passed and my father and I still didn't have a relationship. One day I received a call from Felicia that our father had died. I honestly didn't know how to feel. I was sad to hear that he died, but other than that, I didn't have any emotions. By this time, I was thirty years old and I still didn't know my father. *Was I wrong for having little to no emotions?* I still had so many questions.

I wrestled with whether I was going to go to the funeral or not. I didn't want to attend the funeral and meet a whole new family that I never knew. I wasn't ready for that. Not to mention that my mother had told me that several of my father's family members knew about me as they all worked at the same place for a while. After a few days of thinking, I decided not to go. This was different for me as I always went to my family members' funerals.

Now, of all of my father's children, I stay in contact with Felicia and Marvin, Jr. the most. I see Delano on occasion and chat with him on social media. I finally met my brother, Jamar, at breakfast one Saturday when he approached me and asked, "Are you Brian?" I said, "Yes, and you must be my brother, Jamar." We looked alike. I may never understand why my father was not in my life. I may never know why he was the way he was. I am thankful that at least I met him and his legacy lives on through my siblings and me.

One of the many roles of a father is to teach and protect their children. I am in no way trying to reassign blame; I just wondered how my life would have been with my father in it. *Would I have made some of the decisions that I made? Would I have gotten in trouble with the law? Would I have been on this long road looking for some of the answers that I was looking for? Would I have still ended up behind jail bars?* Who knows? I certainly would have loved to know.

THE WRONG SIDE OF THE BENCH

Even though I was working a full-time job, I still found the time to meet up with my so-called "friends" to hang out and party. I conducted myself in ways that was not consistent with how I was raised and I knew I was wrong. I had just completed the 11th grade in 1993 and I had a 3.97 GPA. However, I still didn't feel like I was understood by any group of people. A part of me wanted to be accepted. I wanted to be around folks that loved me. I kind of lost my own self-worth and value.

One of my so-called "friends" taught me, and another friend, how to obtain fraudulent credit cards. We obtained the cards in other people's names, used them until they were maxed out and then paid the cards off with checks from accounts with insufficient funds. We went from going to the mall periodically, purchasing an item or two, to going to the mall daily using these cards. Grand scheme, right? Wrong!

Our purchases became larger and more frequent. I went from purchasing a tie or belt to thousand-dollar shoes, boots and even jeans that were over $1,200. No, I wasn't on drugs. I had never experimented with drugs (and still haven't), but I was well on my way to a crime-ridden lifestyle. I was completely being a follower and allowing others to manipulate and take advantage of me. This was so not me. The Brian I once knew was no more and I was on a path of total destruction!

In 1998, my life began to spiral. One day, I went to check my mail downstairs in the riverfront apartment that I was living in and, to my surprise, there was a postcard from a district court advising me that I needed to appear in court for a misdemeanor charge. The charge was regarding using checks for an account that had no available funds. "Me? Go to court?" I sweated. I was dumbfounded by what was happening. I guess I thought that I would never get caught or get in trouble.

I called a friend who had been in some trouble before. He warned me of what to expect and offered to go with me to court. When the day came for me to appear, my friend and I went to the courthouse. I was fingerprinted and arraigned before a judge. I was given a personal bond, which meant that I didn't have to put any money up before being released. I was also given another date to return to court.

Honestly, as I think back, even though I had just stood before a judge in open court, I don't think that I thought the matter was as serious as it was. I knew it was serious, but my understanding of how serious didn't rise to the level it should have. This was simply because I truly didn't have any remorse at the time. I don't know why, but I guess reality hadn't set in yet.

When I arrived back to my apartment, I stopped by my mailbox and lo, and behold, there was another notice from another district court advising me that a warrant had been issued for me and that I needed to turn myself in to get the matter resolved. As I made my way to the elevator to go to my apartment, I thought to myself, "Okay, Brian, what have you done?" I was starting to get nervous and concerned that my inappropriate deeds were beginning to catch up with me.

Wow, I had two matters that I needed to clean up and handle now. I started going back and forth to court simultaneously for both matters. Both situations were misdemeanors and I pled guilty to each of them. Then, I was given a period of probation, some court fines, and costs, and a few other conditions ordered by the court. On one of the matters, I received what is called a "diversion" where the offense wouldn't be on my record if I successfully completed all of the requirements ordered by the Court. There was just one condition: I had to attend an economic crimes class.

Jesus, I have to fix this! I cannot go on like this. I was not raised like this. How could I allow myself to get here? I chided myself for days before attending the economic crimes class. There were roughly twenty-five other people in the class from all walks of life. There were several white, privileged teenagers who said they were caught stealing alcohol from Meijer. I also met an Asian woman in her early forties, who, by the way, was wearing a diamond ring that was as big as a quarter. She had become extremely bored because she was a stay-at-home mom so she started going to women's clothing stores and stealing designer labeled clothes. The woman shared that she was so ashamed because her husband was an emergency room doctor and she could afford all of the things that she had been stealing.

I was sitting there thinking to myself, "Wow, so all type of people commit crimes." I then had to introduce myself and share why I was there and what I had done. As I was talking, I began to feel ashamed and embarrassed as there was no good reason why I had done what I did. As the evening went on there were several other activities that the class had to do.

One activity was a group project with four people. I found this project extremely interesting because it showed who was not genuinely accepting responsibility for their actions. My mind was racing and I was growing upset with myself. The reality finally hit me that these were grave matters and that I needed to correct my behavior. Thankfully, I successfully completed both probations and was discharged from each of them.

Still, completing the probations weren't the end. Unfortunately, my employer learned about the convictions and I was terminated. *What am I going to do? I have a car note, rent, and other bills to pay.* I never imagined that I would have gotten myself there. Fortuitously, I did have a little money saved up. Though it wasn't enough to last forever. After about two months, I had fallen behind on my rent and other bills. Before I knew it, I was evicted.

At this point, I had made some of the worst decisions a young person could make. I dropped out of school (almost at the end, mind you). I gave into peer pressure and found myself convicted of economic crimes. After being arrested, evicted, and losing everything, eventually I lost all hope and my self-esteem plummeted. I finally realized that I had altered my life, impacted the reputation of my family, and diverted from the course toward my career path. My plan was clear: go to college, graduate from law school, become a prominent attorney, and end my career on the bench as an officer of the court. But I kept finding myself on the wrong side of the bench!

I know first-hand what it's like to be low on cash and unable to find employment. It's depressing. I thought life was decidedly over for me. I reached out to a couple of friends and explained that I needed to make some money to eat and pay my bills. One of my friends mentioned that he had a way that I could make some quick money and get myself out of debt. I quickly replied, "Let's do it!" without asking any questions.

We began purchasing gift cards from different stores and going back into the stores to make a minimum purchase just to receive the balance on the card given to us in cash. We could literally take a $100 gift card, go into the store, make a $2 purchase, and receive $98 back in cash. After about seven or eight purchases, I had enough money to catch up on my bills.

The problem was that these were credit cards that were obtained illegally. We used other people's information to get the credit cards. I knew this was wrong, but I continued to do it. I felt like my back was up against the wall and I had no other choice. I was too embarrassed to call and ask for help from my grandfather or my mother.

Our crimes grew from small gift cards to opening up large credit cards at designer department stores. We would purchase designer handbags, clothing, and other items with the fraudulent credit cards and then later sell it all for cash. We would then split the proceeds. Some of the people who were buying the items from us were prominent people and they knew that the items were obtained through illegal means. Before I knew it, I was making four times as much money doing this than when I was working every day. Well, all that came to an end… quickly.

One day, while we were at the mall indulging in our misdeeds, we were stopped by mall security as we were exiting the store. The store loss prevention had been watching us all along. Interestingly enough, there was something different about this day. I had a very strange feeling something was going to happen.

When I entered the department store, one of the saleswomen saw I was away from my friends and she asked me, "Why are you with those people?" She said that I did not belong there with them. She recalled assisting me for a long time with my purchases and that I didn't need to be doing what I was doing. I looked at her, perplexed, and did not know what to do or say so I just walked away.

Shortly thereafter, the Troy police arrived and arrested me and my friends. The police read the Miranda Warning, stating our rights, placed us in handcuffs, and took us to the police station. We were all processed into jail and arraigned on multiple charges by the judge. I remember standing before the judge and hearing him give my first friend a bond of $150,000 because he had an extensive criminal background. The judge moved on to my next friend and gave him a $100,000 bond because he had several warrants for his arrest and had not attended court in the past. It was unnerving waiting to hear how much my bond was going to be.

When it was my time to be arraigned, the judge looked at my sheet and saw that I did not have any felonies, but I did have the one misdemeanor that was on my record. He also saw that I had a decent work history in the past and, mentioned on the record, that according to my rap sheet, I was the lesser of three evils. The judge then ordered my bond at $60,000 cash. That's right cash. I rationalized this quickly, "I might as well make this my home because there's no way I'm going to get out of this." At that moment, I was officially ashamed and embarrassed. *How was I going to call home and tell my grandfather this?* Tears began to fall down my face. This could not be happening to me.

After that, we were all taken back to our individual jail cells. When I got in my cell, I immediately went over to the phone in my cell and called my grandfather. I didn't know what I was going to say, but I knew that even if he was mad at me, he was going to come and get me, someway, somehow. When I called my grandfather's house, my step-aunt, Kim, answered the phone. She was living at my grandfather's house at the time. She quickly placed my grandfather on the phone and I told him that I was in jail.

My grandfather asked me how much my bond was and I told him it was $60,000. "Sixty dollars? Okay, I'm on my way," he said.

"No! Sixty thousand dollars," I corrected him.

"Six hundred, Brian?" he asked for clarification again.

"No... sixty... thousand... dollars," I replied to him, slowly.

"Sixty thousand dollars?! What the hell have you done? Killed someone?"

"No, I haven't killed anyone. I was at the mall with some friends and got arrested. We were somewhat... stealing."

"You're going to have to sit your ass there till morning 'cause the credit union closes in a few!"

My grandfather took a deep breath. I gasped. I couldn't believe what I was hearing, but then I could. *Wait a minute! Where did my grandfather have $60,000 at? Why didn't I know this?* I explained to my grandfather that if I wasn't bonded out by 6:00 p.m., he would have to come and get me from the county jail in Pontiac. You would have thought I said Florida instead of Pontiac, Michigan. My grandfather hardly ever drove the expressway and he knew that it would take him forever. "Thank you, Granddaddy, I'll be waiting," I responded, remorsefully. He responded gently, "I know."

A little after 6:00 p.m. everyone who was not bonded out was placed on a van and taken to Oakland County Jail. This was an experience I never wanted to have again. As we exited the van and walked into the jail all shackled together, there were several large cells with at least twenty people in each. The deputies were stationed in the middle around computers and their work areas. One by one, we were fingerprinted, we had our photos taken, we were given a wrist band for identification, and we were placed in a holding cell.

When I got to my holding cell I walked in and said, "What's up?" to everyone and sat on the cement block. There were roughly eight other men in the cell. Several of them looked like they hadn't showered in days and a couple of them seemed to be coming off of a drug or alcohol high. Most of the men in the cell spoke back except for one who was asleep. I looked to the back of the cell and noticed a phone and decided to call my grandfather again. It was around 9:00 p.m. then and I knew that he probably was in the bed asleep.

I dialed the number and after a few rings, shockingly, he answered the phone. I told him that I was at the Oakland County Jail and that's where he should pick me up. "Okay, hang tight. The credit union opens at 9 a.m." He told me that he should be able to get me by 10:30 a.m. "Thank you. I'm sorry," I replied. My grandfather never responded. He simply hung up the phone. I knew he was upset. I grabbed the blanket that was given to me and found a corner on the cell floor and sat there until I fell asleep.

On Friday, April 2, 1998, I woke up at 6:30 a.m. in the Oakland County Jail. The guards were serving breakfast. I looked at what was on the menu and politely offered the dry toast, juice, and oatmeal to whoever wanted it in the cell. I kept the apple to put something on my stomach as I hadn't eaten since the morning before. Several other guys gladly accepted the food that I was giving away. The next thing I know, I was being called to go see the classification department. This is where they asked you a bunch of questions, determined your security level, gave you your jail clothing, and assigned you to the unit you would be housed in.

The lady assisting me was very kind and polite. She affirmed that I looked like I didn't belong there. I admitted that I didn't. She informed me that they were placing me in a low-level housing unit and instructed me to grab a pair of orange pants and shirt in my size. "Do I have to? My grandfather is coming to get me," I appealed. She paused for a minute and said, "I get off at 4:00 p.m. and if your grandfather hasn't come by then, you will have to put them on then and go to your unit." I thanked her and she sent me back to my holding cell.

When I arrived back to the cell everyone was up and talking. I found a spot on the floor and patiently waited. From where I was sitting, I could see the wall clock. After about an hour, I heard the guard walking up the long hallway with his keys rattling. I looked at the clock and it was 10:47 a.m. I immediately stood up and walked up to the front of the cell. When the guard got to the cell and saw me standing there, he asked, "Are you 'Banks'?" I quickly said, "Yes!" "Come with me. You're being bonded out." I was so happy because my grandfather came to get me despite the fact that I was in Pontiac.

I went to the discharge area and had to go through a process. Finally, they lifted the door, told me when my next court date was, and urged me not to come back. I was happy as happy can be! When the gate lifted, I saw my grandfather, Uncle Alvin, and my uncle, Rayford. I was both happy and embarrassed. I was happy to get out of jail, but embarrassed that I was in jail and that I had to tell them what for. No one said a word. We all just started walking out of the entry door to the car.

While we were in the car driving home, I was in the back of the car with my head hung low in shame. I had embarrassed myself and my family. *Why did I do this?* I couldn't believe it. Uncle Alvin asked me what the conditions were like in the jail. I mumbled an answer and quickly lowered my head. I was seated directly behind my grandfather in the car. My grandfather looked in the rear-view mirror and said to me, "Hold your head up! You're still going to be a lawyer." *WHAT?! How could I even get into law school now? Humph, I'll be a lesser known lawyer.* We continued home with very little conversation.

When we finally arrived at my grandfather's house, he and I sat at the kitchen table. He asked me, "What happened?" I told him everything and he immediately started giving me a tongue lashing. My grandfather began cursing and conjugating subject verb agreements like no one else could. It seemed like he was never going to stop. He told me that he found an attorney and we were going to see him on Monday morning. I thanked him again and expressed my sorrowfulness.

We went to the attorney's office on Monday. My grandfather went in his pocket and counted out the attorney's retainer. My grandfather looked at me and said, "You're going to pay me every penny back." I immediately said, "Yes, sir." From there, my frequent court dates started and I was eventually bound over to circuit court on multiple felony charges. This meant that my case was going to be heard in the circuit court because they were felonies and carried a possible penalty of more than 93 days in jail.

Revelation Day

I learned that my criminal case would be held in the Oakland County Circuit Court. My friend, Tori, had experience with the criminal justice system in Oakland County, so I asked her about it. She hoped I would be assigned to Judge Denise Langford Morris's courtroom. Tori found Judge Langford Morris to be a very fair, respectful, and diligent judge. Tori also explained that Judge Langford Morris was the only black judge on the bench at the Oakland County Circuit Court.

After waiting a couple of weeks, I finally received a notice in the mail stating what day and time I had to report to court. When I looked over the entire notice, I saw that I was assigned to Judge Denise Langford Morris. I began to wonder if I would receive the same treatment that Tori expressed during her ordeal. Tori shared with me that Judge Langford Morris was a very nice lady and that she seemed to care about everyone who came before her in court regardless of what their matter involved. Only time would tell. My attorney later reached out to let me know that I had an upcoming court date and to meet him outside of the courtroom on that day.

My first court appearance at the circuit court was a very brief hearing as it was simply an arraignment on the information. My grandfather and Uncle Alvin accompanied me to the hearing. The judge read my charges in open court and I was given notice of my next few court appearances. There was the judge – this tall, beautiful, black lady in a long, black robe. It was Judge Denise Langford Morris.

She spoke in a respectful tone each and every person that came before her. There seemed to be nine or ten cases before mine and then, finally, my case was called. After my hearing, my attorney spoke to me and my family in the hall to describe the next steps. He advised that he would be speaking with the prosecutor to see if he could work out some type of plea deal. My next court appearance wasn't for three weeks and my attorney explained that he will be in contact with me soon.

One day I decided to do some research on Judge Langford Morris. To my surprise, I found countless articles about the judge and her numerous accomplishments. I was quite impressed to see that she was born and raised in the city of Detroit and attended Detroit Public Schools. I was also fascinated to learn that she had started her career in social work and then went on to become an attorney and then a judge. *That's what I want to do!*

A defining moment of my life came on a fateful day in 1999, when I stood before Oakland County Circuit Court Judge Denise Langford Morris. Somehow, standing in front of her, I knew and realized that it was time for me to grasp a hold on my life. I remember the judge speaking life into me and seeing something on the inside of me that I did not even know still existed — GREATNESS! Judge Langford Morris encouraged me to utilize my brilliance in a positive manner, to go to school, and get on the straight path.

I was a little bit nervous about my next court hearing as I did not know what to expect. When I arrived to the court room it was packed with attorneys and their clients waiting for their cases to be called. *It is 1:30 p.m. We're going to be here forever! The judge will never get through all these cases before five o'clock.* This was such an eye-opening time for me. The court proceedings finally got my attention.

There was something about the lady in the long, black robe that was frightening and yet alluring. For me, judges were intimidating and didn't really seem to genuinely care about the well-being of those who stood before them. At this time in my life, judges seemed to care more about executing judgment, however, that was not the case with Judge Denise Langford Morris. Fortunately, as the judge called each case, she spent time listening and understanding each matter, and then, respectfully and professionally, ruled on each one in a very expeditious manner.

"People of the State of Michigan versus Brian Banks," the court clerk announced my case. My attorney, Mr. Condino, was dressed in a navy blue suit, arose and I, dressed in a black suit, quickly followed him up to the podium. My attorney stated his name and bar license number so that the court stenographer could put it in the transcript. Judge Langford Morris spoke with both my attorney and the prosecuting attorney. She asked the attorneys if they had worked out any type of plea deal. Both attorneys asked if they could approach the bench and the judge allowed them.

I was left standing at the podium alone while my attorney and the prosecutor were speaking with the judge. *What are they saying?* The judge only seemed to listen and eventually she said, "Thank you." Both lawyers walked back to the podium where I was standing. Judge Langford Morris said she was adjourning the matter for three weeks to allow the attorneys an opportunity to come up with a deal.

I was totally shocked. My hearing lasted every bit of three minutes. *You mean to tell me I drove an hour from my house to the courthouse and was only there for three minutes?! I sat in this courtroom for hours only to have my time over with in three minutes?!* I didn't know what to think. I was perturbed and relieved simultaneously, and still, I was growing a little bit weary as it appeared that my court matter was being strung along.

My attorney, Mr. Condino, took me into the hall and divulged that he was trying to work out the best deal for me with the prosecuting attorney. "Sometimes, Brian, it takes a while before all parties can reach an amicable agreement," he assured me. I was getting a little irritated as I was running out of money. Gas wasn't cheap and the constant back and forth between Wayne County and Oakland County was costing me a pretty penny. I had lost my job once they found out that I had been arrested so my income had stopped and my savings was running low.

My next court date was a week away and I was hoping and praying that by then we would have some resolve. Prior to my court date, Mr. Condino, called to let me know that he had spoken with the prosecutor and that they might have a deal, but we would not know until we arrived to court. A week later at the courthouse, Mr. Condino was already there and waiting in the hallway when I walked in. He shared with me that he and the prosecuting attorney had come up with what he believed to be the best deal for me. Several of the charges were going to be dropped and I would be placed on one-year probation with the first six months wearing a tether in lieu of going to jail. This was not my idea of a fashion statement, but it sure beat being behind prison walls.

Mr. Condino carefully explained everything to me and went over all of the documents. I agreed that this was probably the best offer that I was going to get, but it also was the start of me comprehending that I had to make better choices and better decisions. I did not want to end up here again. I read over all the documents and then signed the plea offer and gave it back to my attorney. We both went and sat inside the court room and waited for my case to be called.

"People of the State of Michigan versus Brian Banks," the clerk yelled out. "Parties are here for a Settlement Conference," she advised the judge. Judge Langford Morris greeted all of us and asked the attorneys to state their appearances for the record and then asked if we had an agreement. Mr. Condino advised the judge that we had an agreement and he began to lay out the terms of the agreement. Judge Langford Morris directed a question to the prosecutor about being aligned with this agreement, to which he replied that he was.

Judge Langford Morris looked at me and said, "Mr. Banks, I understand, through your attorney that you wish to avail yourself of the plea offer that has been extended to you." I replied, "Yes, your honor." If I didn't know anything else, I knew that I needed to give the utmost respect to the judge considering my fate was in her hands. Judge Langford Morris asked me to raise my right hand and she had the clerk to swear me in to tell the truth. Judge Langford Morris went on to ask me a series of questions including: what I had done on the date in question and if I knew what I was doing was wrong and if I had continued that behavior. Judge Langford Morris took her time taking my plea and afterwards she took additional time to share her insight and wisdom with me.

The judge began to tell me that I was too intelligent to make the decisions that I'd been making. She shared that I needed to go back to school and get my GED and go on further with my education. The judge also told me that I needed to stop hanging with the wrong people. She said, "Look, you come from a good family. Your family has been here with you in court. You're well-dressed and well-spoken." Everything the judge was saying really resonated with me.

Even though it was only a two-minute conversation, I felt like the judge put everyone else out of the courtroom and was talking to me as if I was the only person in the room. *It's time to do better. I can't continue down this path.* I told the judge that I appreciated her and her words and that they didn't fall on deaf ears. My next court appearance was in three weeks and that was my sentencing day.

As I drove home, I thought about everything that Judge Langford Morris said to me. Wow! This woman really seemed to care about me. I knew that I needed to do better. I just didn't understand how I allowed everything about me to be deviant, but I was determined to fix one thing; I was going to get my GED before I went back to court.

The next day I looked up information regarding GED testing and went and took the test and passed it on my first attempt. I was so excited and couldn't wait to tell the judge. I called and shared the news with my attorney and he was pleasantly surprised. Both my grandfather and mother were happy that I went and got my GED. I told them that this was just the beginning and I was going to go back to school.

From that day on, I suddenly took the reins of my life and no longer let my hurts, disappointments and failures — my past — dictate my future. I grabbed hold to the encouragement from Judge Langford Morris. I continued to receive support and assistance from my mother and grandfather and, at age 24, I began to turn my life around. That doesn't mean everything was perfect after that. I still had to deal with other matters that came up from my past. It seemed like as soon as I took care of one matter, another matter from my past arose. It was always at the most inconvenient times. One time I had to call my cousin, Debbie, to come and get me out of jail. I was so ready to put all this behind me.

At my sentencing day, Mr. Condino reviewed with me my pre-sentencing report that the probation department completed for the judge. He wanted me to make sure that everything in it was correct. I found that there were no errors. Once my case was called, Mr. Condino and I approached the podium. My attorney began to go over the pre-sentence report and he also shared with the judge that I had received my GED.

"Congratulations!" the judge was pleased. She admonished me to continue my education. She told me to use this experience as a learning experience. The judge honored the plea agreement and sentenced me to one-year probation with the first six months on a tether. Along with that, there were some other conditions like court costs, fines, and restitution. Judge Langford Morris's words really hit home for me. It was time for me to grow up. I did have a lot to offer the world. It was like her words were saving my life. It was the day that I knew I had to change. It was my "Revelation Day."

After a few weeks of searching for a job, I landed employment through a contract company at a foreclosure law firm. However, having the tether on my ankle was causing some problems as I had to be in the house by a certain time each day and my tether agent was not willing to adjust my time so I could work overtime and make some additional money. After all, I had a high restitution bill along with my other bills. I was just trying to get all of this court stuff over with. After a few months, my issues with the tether and my job grew worse. I ended up losing my job because I couldn't work the mandatory overtime. I was pissed!

Here I was trying to do right and I lost my job. See, some folks may think that getting a tether is getting off easy. Well, I'm here to tell you that's not the case. Honestly, the criminal justice system, in its current form, is set up for you to fail. After admitting your guilt and accepting responsibility, you are later assessed a ton of court fines, restitution, and other fees without even having a job. To make matters worse, you are now a felon which, in and of itself, prevents you from getting most jobs. Nevertheless, all these costs have to be paid somehow and, when you don't, you violate your court order and your probation and you can ultimately be put back in jail. It's a vicious cycle!

I tried to find how I could get that tether off of my leg. I contacted Mr. Condino, but when he quoted what he would charge me, I realized that I needed to do this on my own. I did not have any money for an attorney to handle this for me. After researching for weeks, I drafted a motion which I later filed at the court to remove my tether. I had another hearing before Judge Langford Morris and I decided to represent myself.

I explained that the tether was putting me in a bad financial hardship. I showed how much money I was making from my job and shared all of my monthly responsibilities, including the additional money that I was being charged for having the tether. At the end of the hearing, Judge Langford Morris ordered that the tether be removed. "Now," she emphasized, "you need to get back in school and go to someone's law school!" I thanked her for taking the time to speak with me and told her that I was going to make her proud.

As time went by, and as I started my new path of life, I often wondered about Judge Langford Morris and really appreciated the seeds that she sowed in me by not simply judging me, but seeing my potential. When I completed my undergraduate degree, I wanted to reach out to Judge Langford Morris and share with her my accomplishment, but fear got in the way. *What if she doesn't remember me? What if she is mean to me?* I really didn't know what to do and decided on doing nothing. Periodically, I would ask different people if they knew her or had seen her in public as I was hoping to bump into her at an event or restaurant.

Years later, my friend Roeiah and I were talking about our accomplishments and I told her that I really wanted to let Judge Langford Morris know about everything that I had achieved. Unbelievably, Roeiah had met Judge Langford Morris at the hospital while they both were visiting the same patient. They begin to have a conversation and decided to exchange information. Roeiah told me that she was going to reach out to Judge Langford Morris and set up a meeting.

A few days later, Roeiah let me know that she and Judge Langford Morris had spoken and had a lunch date scheduled. Roeiah told me that she asked the judge if one of her friends could join them and the judge agreed. Roeiah said, "Brian, this is your opportunity to let the judge know everything that you've done." Immediately, fear began to rise and I felt unsettled.

I didn't know if it was proper for a prior defendant to show up and have a conversation with his sentencing judge, nor did I know if the judge would be nervous or scared of me. I went back-and-forth on whether I was going to go to the lunch or not. At the last minute, I decided to go and meet Roeiah and the judge. I jumped in my car and drove to Brandy's, a restaurant on Telegraph in Pontiac, where Roeiah and Judge Langford Morris were meeting. Upon my arrival, the waitress took me to the table where Roeiah, Judge Langford Morris, and another young lady were sitting at the table talking. As I approached the table, I greeted everyone and then extended my hand to the judge. I was wondering if she would remember me. At no time did she act as if she knew me or acknowledge if I even looked familiar.

I ordered my lunch and sat and listened to the conversation that was taking place at the table. Judge Langford Morris was describing her morning docket to Roeiah and the other young lady and the various cases that she had heard. Roeiah and the young lady had observed the judge while she was on the bench hearing her morning cases. The judge pointed out that she often tries to encourage young people to do the right thing, such as, going back to school and furthering their educations. The judge then described the case of a young man who was sentenced earlier that day in her court room. Listening to Judge Langford Morris, I marveled because the entire story of that young man reminded me of myself. I was thinking that she was talking about me. The entire story sounded so familiar.

I sat and listened to the judge thinking that it was the perfect time for me to chime in and thank her for believing in me and giving me another opportunity. When the opportunity presented itself, I interjected and said, "Judge, I think this is the perfect time for me to tell you, 'thank you'. Seven and a half years ago I stood before you as a lost, young, black male with multiple felony charges. While I was going through the process, I really didn't understand why you were adjourning my matter and having us come back, but later I found out that it was to allow the attorneys the opportunity to work out a plea deal. Not knowing the process, I had become frustrated and slightly angry because of all the back-and-forth and all of the money that I didn't have that it was costing me. You handled me with the utmost respect and professionalism. You did not judge me and, even though you had to execute judgment, you did it with a sense of respect and not in a demeaning nature. I thank you for that."

I told her that she saw something in me that I didn't know still existed in me; that was greatness! I expressed my appreciation to her for giving me another chance and I wanted her to know that that chance did not go to waste. I concluded by announcing to her, "As of today, while we are in this restaurant, I have my bachelor's and master's degrees and I am currently in my first year of law school. I took the opportunity that you gave me and tried to make the best of it. Thank you!"

Judge Langford Morris was totally shocked. She sat at the table right across for me with tears welling up in her eyes while I spoke. She told me that no litigant had ever come back with a story like mine. She explained how proud she was of me and all of my accomplishments. She was astounded that she had had that much impact on my life. I further inquired with her if she still had the same staff because I remembered that every time I came in contact with them, they were professional and respectful. She indeed had the same staff and invited me to come back to the courthouse after lunch to see them. She said she couldn't wait to share with them my good news.

When we arrived to Judge Langford Morris' courtroom, I was greeted by two of her staff members. One of them said, "You look familiar." Judge Langford Morris asked her staff if they remembered Brian Banks. One of her staffers said,

"Yes!" infatuatedly, and looked at me, asked how I was doing and what I had been doing. It was a good experience to be able to go back and express my gratitude to the judge and her staff. I promised Judge Langford Morris and her staff that I would keep in contact with them. They were all so supportive of the vision I had for my life. This meant the world to me as I knew having a support system was extremely important.

As the years went by, I made good on my promise and maintained contact with Judge Langford Morris. I began to invite her to several events, especially those events hosted by the Black law students at my law school. Judge Langford Morris graciously accepted the invitations and attended many of the events.

When I graduated from law school, Judge Langford Morris and several other judges and friends treated me to dinner to celebrate. By this time, Judge Langford Morris was pursuing a run for the Michigan Supreme Court. I, without hesitation, volunteered to assist and work on her campaign. I knew a little bit about campaigning from my friend, Judge Vonda Evans, so I thought this would be a great opportunity for me to learn more and to meet new people. In all of my endeavors this judge had been the most supportive and a constant role model. Volunteering on Judge Langford Morris's Supreme Court campaign afforded me a great opportunity, plus it allowed the judge and I to foster a great mentor/mentee relationship which still exists to this day.

One thing that I will always remember about Judge Langford Morris is her commitment to education. During many of my court hearings in her courtroom, I can remember her telling other defendants, whose matters were being heard before mine, to get in school, to further their education and to stay in school. I can recall a quote from Horace Mann that says, "Education, then, beyond all other devices of human origin, is the great equalizer of the conditions of men, the balance-wheel of the social machinery." This rings true for me as education has been one of my main driving forces and catalyst for my personal growth and change. However, getting that education was not as easy as I had hoped.

School and the Extra Push

My ninth and tenth grade years were good as far as my grades were concerned. For the most part, I kept all A's. Socially, I tried to make the best of it. I wanted to start a gospel choir at the high school and the school administration took me through the ringer.

One of my favorite things to do was go to church. My mother kept me in church every Sunday and I became involved with many of the organizations and departments within the church. As a result, I grew an appreciation for good, gospel music. Even at school, some of my friends and I would walk down the halls singing church songs until the teachers told us to quiet down. With all of the fighting and chaos going on in the school, I thought that a gospel choir would be a perfect distraction for us. It seemed like I had to speak to everybody who was somebody to make something like that happen. When I spoke to the assistant principal, he told me I needed to speak to the principal.

While I was sitting in the principal's office, I looked at him and said, "I don't mean any disrespect, but I've been here three years and I don't even know who you are." This was the first time I had even laid eyes on this guy. I had never seen him walk the halls and you know he didn't deal with the things we dealt with on a daily basis. I mean, my locker had been broken into several times. My mother bought me a polo jacket and someone stole it. There were just so many bad things going on in school, including gangs and violence. To make it worse, at home, nothing changed. We still had issues with Rose. It was at that time I began to rethink and rehash those remarks she said the night of the last fight. I was tired of it.

Even though there was turmoil in the school's music department, I finally got a sponsor and the approval for the gospel choir to start. The music department teachers did not like how I had around sixty or seventy students that came out to participate in the gospel choir rehearsals compared to the regular concert choir. None of the school choirs had as many students as the gospel choir. It seemed that they tried to find a reason to stop us from having the choir. It became the hot spot after school especially for us "church kids" who loved to sing.

Our gospel choir rehearsals reminded many of us of church. There were some really good singers involved. It was also really amazing that three of us played the piano and several others played other instruments. We didn't care what denomination everyone was from. We just loved singing. After a successful spring concert debut, we began to get engagement requests to sing at different churches, schools, and events. It seemed like every week we were met with a problem or someone trying to disband us.

At the end of the semester we had a huge concert and it helped to bring the entire school together. Unfortunately, we were told that because the other choirs didn't have the adequate participation levels that we would not be allowed to have the gospel choir the next school year. Sadly, they were successful in shutting us down.

When the next semester started, school wasn't the same. It seemed like there was no morale, no interest, and that the teachers really didn't care. Some of our teachers from the last semester had retired or went to other schools, causing us to have some new teachers. I became bored, uninterested, and not challenged. To add insult to injury, things still weren't better at home.

I soon developed the bad habit of skipping school. My grandfather had finally retired and was able to drive me to school every day. When my grandfather would drop me off at school, I would leave the school and catch the bus and make it back home before he did. There was not a teacher, an administrator, or anyone who caught me. I was under the radar. Absolutely no one questioned where I was for several weeks.

The school finally called my home and asked where I had been. Mrs. Brantley was someone who had really taken to me. She was also the sponsor for the gospel choir. She noticed that she hadn't seen me and started inquiring of other teachers. My family didn't know that I had been skipping school either. When I got off of the bus and made it back home, I would stop in the kitchen, make me something to eat, and stay in my room all day until my grandfather would leave to go pick up Rose from work. When they came home, I would be downstairs like I had just come home from school and that went on for weeks.

I finally sat down and told my mother and my grandfather that I didn't want to go to school so I was dropping out. They didn't understand. They asked me why and I couldn't give them a good answer. "I just don't want to go back anymore," I said. They took me out of public school and put me in a private school called Lutheran East High School. I was challenged just a little bit more, but by this time, I just couldn't get it together. Mentally, I wasn't there anymore. I had checked out.

I knew my mother loved me, I knew my grandfather loved me and I know that they did the best they could. I just decided school wasn't the place for me at that point in my life.

So, I started skipping again and I ended up just leaving school period. I ultimately dropped out of school in the 11th grade with a 3.97 GPA.

My grandfather was disappointed with me and told me that I couldn't live in his house if I didn't go to school or work. He said if I wasn't going to school then I needed to get a job. I thought to myself, "No problem, I will get a job," and that's just what I did. I worked several places before I landed a good paying job at AAA Michigan. I entered the workforce with a limited education, but still managed to bring home $900 every two weeks after taxes (and this was in 1993).

After working at AAA, I found out that Ameritech was hiring. It was a better opportunity for me and it was a unionized job. I applied for the job and got it. Not long after that, I thought to myself, "I need to go back and at least get a GED." (This was while I was waiting for my sentencing day.) I researched where I could get my GED from and scheduled a time to take the test.

Upon my arrival at the testing location, the lady asked me where I had been studying for the test. I explained that I hadn't been studying, but rather I had been working. She explained that most folks need to study for a period of time before they're able to pass the test. I retorted that I appreciated her feedback, but I simply wanted to take the test. She then got on her soapbox to try and discourage me from taking the test without studying. Needless to say, I took the test and passed it with flying colors. I only missed one question and it was in social studies. That was never my favorite subject anyway.

Obtaining my GED was a small accomplishment, but I still loved learning and missed several things about school. I decided to enroll at Wayne County Community College and take several courses there. I easily passed my classes and, after two semesters, one of my adjunct professors suggested that I look into Wayne State University. She shared with me a program at Wayne State University called, "College of Lifelong Learning." This program was for the non-traditional student. I called and made an appointment with an advisor. A few days later, I went to visit the College of Lifelong Learning.

After learning more about the program, I applied and was accepted on the spot. The advisor registered me for my first two classes at Wayne State University. "Wow!" I thought, "I am actually about to start college. I am actually about to be a college student." I called and told my mother and grandfather about my decision to go back to school to work on my bachelor's degree. Both of them were very happy and proud that I decided to further my education.

Shortly after my acceptance, the semester started and I was on my way. I had gone to the bookstore and purchased my books and supplies. I was ready to begin this new chapter in my life. After a few weeks into my courses I thought to myself, "Wow, I have the hang of this, I can do this." I began to think about what my educational goals were. *What am I going to major in? What do I want to be?* One of my professors told me that the answers to those questions would come along if I just continued to work hard and get acclimated to the school/ university process. She advised me to work on my general education requirements and that I had time to decide what my major was going to be.

Before I knew it, I had knocked out both my midterm and final exams and ultimately passed my first two courses at Wayne State University. I later went to my advisor and he registered me for my next set of courses but, instead of two courses this semester, I decided to take three. It was through those classes that I began to form friendships with other students who came from all walks of life.

About three semesters in, I decided that I would apply to the mortuary science school. After all, I had been working part-time at a funeral home for number of years and was already doing many of the jobs there from making arrangements with families, to playing the organ, to driving the hearse and had performing many other responsibilities. I thought this would fit in perfectly. I was already doing the work. I thought I'd get a degree behind my name and then open up my own funeral home.

I went to declare my Major to be Mortuary Science and discovered the number of pre-requisite classes that I needed to take prior to be admitted into the program. I began this journey of taking prerequisites for mortuary science, however, I soon discovered that there was no burning in my belly for mortuary science. I begin to think to myself, "Is this really a passion? Is this really what I wanted to do with my life?" I would have had to take several classes without being totally enthused. I quickly decided mortuary science was not for me.

Through my very own experience, my interest was heightened in criminal justice since I had witnessed first-hand the many disparities that existed in the system. I had observed defendants being incarcerated because they were poor, those who couldn't afford bail, and I even noticed some court appointed attorneys pressuring defendants into pleading guilty because of their client caseload.

This infuriated me and caused me to want to further my education in criminal justice. I decided one day that I wanted to be a lawyer, and then, a judge. I began to chart out what the best path for me would be to change my major to Criminal Justice. I later went to the Criminal Justice Department at the University and applied. I was accepted and that's when I began to nurture my passion for the law.

Once I started taking criminal justice courses, I began to meet many people who worked in the field — lawyers, probation officers, judges, law-enforcement officers, and many others. I began to develop so many great friendships and relationships with other classmates. Several special bonds were made with classmates and we began to take all of our classes together each semester so that we had a support system. I was even awarded a scholarship from the Howard Baker Foundation as a result of my hard work and good grades.

After three and a half years of diligence I was finally ready to graduate with my Bachelor's Degree in Criminal Justice from Wayne State University. I could not believe that I had gone back to school and accomplished this goal of getting my bachelor's degree. After all, I was the first one in my immediate family to obtain a bachelor's degree. I did not allow any of my failures, setbacks, and disappointments to stand in the way of me reaching this goal.

The excitement and happiness on both my mother's and grandfather's faces, when I told them that I was graduating, was priceless! I made both of them proud. I told my grandfather that I wanted to be a lawyer and from that point forward he began to call me "Sam Bernstein". At the time, Sam Bernstein was one of the only lawyers who advertised on TV regularly and my grandfather had become accustomed to seeing and hearing his name.

The day of my graduation was so special. I was among well over 1,500 other graduates in Cobo Hall and, as my name was called, and I walked across the stage, I could hear my family and friends cheering me on and yelling my name from the rafters. This was one of the greatest moments of my life. My grandfather, mother, brother, Step-aunt Jackie, my cousin, Debbie, and one of my friends, Keith, were all there to see me graduate from college.

After that, I had to figure out what I was going to do next. I needed to make some money to pay my bills, but I realized I had a few obstacles in the way, especially my criminal convictions. While I was working on my bachelor's degree, I started substitute teaching to earn income. After my graduation, I landed a teaching job at a charter school where I was supposed to be the building substitute and then a Spanish teacher. However, there was a teacher shortage and, two days before classes started, I was told I was going to be teaching third grade.

Even though I was teaching, I never lost sight of becoming an attorney and then a judge. I had to make money and pay my bills, but also needed to enjoy what I was doing at the moment. As I began to teach third grade, I fell in love with all of my students and their learning abilities. I became very engaged, quite active in the school culture and environment, and began to volunteer on many committees to provide a well-rounded, adequate education for all students. Through that, one of my administrators began to see my leadership abilities and asked me, "Why don't you start working on your Master's degree in Educational Leadership?"

If I do that, I'll never get to law school. If I get my Master's in Educational Leadership, would it help me to make more money? Would it further prolong my dream and goal of law school? I had a lot of questions and no answers. I began to speak with some colleagues of mine at the school who were working on their Master's degrees and, as they shared their personal stories, I decided to give it a try. I enrolled at Wayne State University in the College of Education to get my Master's in Education & Administration.

Even during my graduate studies, I often found myself thinking about law school. I attended events for prospective law students and those who had an interest in the field of law. I also began to attend fundraisers for judges and judicial candidates and other legal events in an attempt to associate myself with those already working in the field of law. I realized that teaching school and the education field of study was only a stepping-stone to my law career.

After completing my Master's degree, it was time for another graduation. I was not entirely enthused to go to my graduation because this was really not my passion. My grandfather insisted that I had to go. After all, it was sunny and eighty degrees in May in the city of Detroit. At my graduation from grad school sat my grandfather, my mother, my brother, and my friends, Angie, Beverly, and Joe. The ceremony seemed like it was never going to end. I was so over it. After the graduation ceremony we decided to have lunch at J Alexander's restaurant.

While at lunch my friend, Angie, asked, "What's next for you?" It was at that time that I decided that someway, somehow, law school had to be next. I explained that I believed I could make a difference because going through the tumultuous times and process in the criminal justice system, I saw firsthand the inequities in the system, and I saw what the system can do to those who aren't aware of how it works. I explained that I wanted to help the poor, the disenfranchised, and those with no voice. That was my passion — law, the study of law, and the criminal justice system.

I heard several times that I would never get accepted into law school because of my past decisions and mistakes. After all, I was a convicted felon. Conversely, I had also heard of the story of Judge Greg Mathis, who made some poor choices and decisions in his youth. When he was young, he was arrested, and still went to law school and became a prominent attorney and TV judge. His story gave me hope. I hoped that if God did it for him, he could do it for me. *I know that it will be an uphill battle, but who is more capable of the battle than me?*

I began to research the process for getting accepted into law school. I discovered that the first step was taking and getting a decent score on the LSAT, which was the law school admissions test. I began to look for study programs and classes that helped prepare students to take the LSAT. I soon discovered that, the cost of these programs were out of my price range. I went to my local bookstore and purchased an LSAT prep book so that I could begin studying on my own. After a few weeks of studying, I thought to myself, "I will never be able to do this." It seemed as if I wasn't making any progress.

I later found out about an eight-session weekend program, which was in my price range, to study for the LSAT. I enrolled in the course and attended the sessions every Saturday. The sessions helped me tremendously. I felt that I could conquer the exam. The only problem was that I really did not like taking standardized tests. I had to mentally and emotionally prepare for this.

After completing the course, it was time to register to take the real exam. After registering, I remember waking up that Saturday morning feeling nauseous and scared. I did not want to do it, but I realized I had to do it. I arrived at the University of Detroit Mercy law school to take the LSAT exam with several hundred other students. The room was cold and the floor was squeaky; the building was old. I remember repeating to myself, "You can do this! You can do this!" After several hours of torture, I had completed the LSAT. Now the real torture began as I waited for my results.

After several weeks of waiting, my LSAT results finally arrived. I was a bit nervous to open them, but I finally decided to open the envelope. When I opened the envelope, I saw that I had scored less than what I was aiming for, but it wasn't the absolute worse. I contemplated on retaking the exam, but later learned that both scores would be averaged out and that could hurt me in the end. After speaking with a few law school admission counselors and reading a few blogs, I decided that I would keep the score that I had, but focus on preparing a strong application package. After all, I had a good undergraduate GPA and many life experiences that the traditional student would not have.

I carefully began the arduous task of researching law schools and their admissions process. A lot of schools that I wanted to attend were out of my league due to my low LSAT score. There were times that I grew frustrated and discouraged because I thought it would never happen for me. I would find a school and it would be miles and miles away with a much harder admissions process than I was up for. In addition to the admissions process, there were enormous fees that were required to submit with your law school application. That was money I did not have. The more and more I researched, the more and more I became discouraged and defeated.

For weeks, it seemed that my daily routine was searching the Internet, making calls to law school admission offices, leaving messages, and working on my law school personal statement. When I began my personal statement, I did not know what was too much to tell and what was not enough. The task of telling my personal story in my statement became harder and harder. My thought process was, "If I tell this, will they look at me a particular way?" or "If I tell that, how will they view me?" I wanted to share all of the obstacles and roadblocks that I faced to show that I had the capacity to pursue the rigorous study of law, but I did not want to tell too much for fear of being embarrassed and ashamed.

After talking this over with my grandfather, it was clear that he did not want me to go out of state to attend law school. Quiet as it was kept, I really didn't care if I went out of state or stayed in state. I just wanted to go to law school. It was then that I started to reel my focus into all of the Michigan law schools and the programs they offered. I looked at University of Michigan Law School, Ave Maria Law School, which was in Michigan at the time, University of Detroit Mercy Law School, Wayne State Law School, Michigan State University College of Law, and Cooley Law School.

I begin to apply and no sooner than I applied, the denial letters started to come. After the second denial letter, I started to second-guess myself and wonder if this really was for me. I remember being on the campus of Wayne State and stopping by the law school and speaking with a former dean there about law school admissions. She looked at my undergraduate transcripts and my LSAT and said I would be a great fit. However, when I went on to tell her about my life story and the obstacles that I had faced, she acquiesced that it would be a hard road ahead.

She also asked me if I really wanted three degrees from the same institution. *What does it matter as long as I have the degrees?*

Several weeks went by and I continued to apply and wait on decision letters. After my fourth denial letter I began to say, "What's the use?" I thought all was lost and I thought it would never happen for me. I recall having a conversation with a friend who told me, "Brian, what God has for you is for you and, if it's God's will for you to attend law school, it will happen. It will happen in God's time, not yours." I had to take a step back and realize that if it was meant to be, it was going to be, despite all of my mishaps.

One day while lying in bed, I remember the conversation I had with a lady named Linda, who answered the phone at Michigan State University College of Law when I had to call the college to get some information. Linda was different from the others I had spoken with at other schools as she was patient, informative, and encouraging. Even though I didn't know her, I felt a sense of calmness while speaking with her as it related to my past and my desire to go to law school. She confessed to me about one of her life hurdles and obstacles that she was able to overcome. She also shared that she was currently enrolled in school at Michigan State University. I thought to myself, "I want to call and have another conversation with her."

I hesitantly called the school and had another very good conversation with Linda. She encouraged me to visit and take a tour of the law school campus. Linda explained that I would be able to sit in some law school classes, as well as meet some professors and students. I was really unsure if I wanted to face another defeat, but I reluctantly agreed to make the appointment. I asked if my friend, Roeiah, could join me as I was aware of her desire to attend law school and become an attorney as well. Roeiah and I grew up in the same neighborhood and attended elementary and high school together. "Sure, please bring her," Linda said, "I look forward to seeing you next week."

"Roeiah, I'm going to give it another shot and visit Michigan State University College of Law. I made arrangements for both of us to visit and take a tour next week," I said, when I called Roeiah to give her the good news. "I'll take off work that day and drive us," she said, excitedly. As the days got closer for us to go Lansing, Michigan, I became less and less interested. I didn't want to face another "no". I didn't want to have to go through telling my story, including all of my bad choices in life. I didn't want to have to face my past again. At that point, I really didn't know if I should go or not.

The day before we were scheduled to go to the school, Roeiah called to confirm she was driving and would be at my house at a certain time the next day. I told her I was having second thoughts and really didn't know if I wanted to go. "What do you have to lose?" Roeiah asked, and then stated matter-of-factly, "We're going!" I told her I'd call her in the morning when I woke up to let her know my final decision.

When I woke up the next day it was pouring down raining, gloomy, and a bit chilly. It put me in a very blah and depressive mood. "Oh no, I cannot go to the law school today," I said to myself. I picked up my phone to call Roeiah to tell her I wasn't going to be able to go. She answered the phone and said, "I don't care what you're saying. We're going. I will be there at 10:30 a.m. to pick you up."

I thought to myself, "Why did I do this? What have I gotten myself into? How am I going to get out of this? Do I really want to go through with this?" I finally got myself out of the bed and jumped in the shower to prepare for the day. As the time drew closer for her to pick me up, my nerves got the best of me. I got dressed and turned on the TV.

There was a story on about a young lady who was trying to start a company. Everywhere she went for assistance, such as a loan, supplies, and other things, she was told, "No." She went to her family for help. They told her "no." She went to the bank and they told her "no". The young lady began to share that a mentor of hers told her never to accept the word "no". She said, "If someone tells you 'no' at the front door, go to the back door. If they tell you 'no' at the back door, go to the side door. If they tell you 'no' at the side door, get a ladder and go up to the window." I took that story and I applied it to where I was at the time regarding getting accepted into law school. I did not know how, but I knew that taking the trip to MSU was going to pay off at some point.

Roeiah pulled up to my house in her Chevy Tahoe. I made a mad dash from my front door to keep from getting wet and jumped into her truck. During our entire ride from Detroit to Lansing, Roeiah and I began to talk about our childhood and growing up on Camden and Hampshire. We reminisced about our elementary school days. We talked about our families and our home environments while growing up. We started thanking God for everything that we were able to overcome as children and even then as adults.

Roeiah was a recently divorced mother of two and was working a full-time job for the State of Michigan. Roeiah and I both grew up in church and loved God and Gospel music. On our ride, Roeiah had on repeat a CD of Shekinah Glory Ministry. After about the first 30 minutes, I told her to turn it off because I was tired of listening to the same songs. We both laughed and let the CD continue to play.

We stopped on our way and grabbed something to eat and filled up for gas. The hour and fifteen-minute drive seemed like eternity. I didn't think we would ever get through the rain and get to the law school for our tour. When we arrived on the campus of Michigan State University, my heart began to beat faster and faster. I became extremely nervous. I had to sit there in the passenger seat and act as if nothing was wrong. I had to tell myself that I could do this, and that this was going to be the one.

Upon our arrival to the Law School, we went to the admissions office and the first person who greeted us was Miss Linda, the lady who I had spoken with over the phone several times. She welcomed us to the law school and asked if we had any trouble finding it. We told her "no" and that we were glad to be there. Miss Linda gave us some brochures and explained what was going to take place during our tour. She already had a student waiting to take us around and explain to us all of the different programs, classes, and activities at the law school.

During the tour, our student tour guide took us into an actual law school class. We were allowed to sit in the back of the class to hear the professor and the students during their classroom learning experience. This was totally new to me. It was exciting! I could see myself sitting there, but I just didn't know how it was going to happen. What was interesting during the tour was that Roeiah and I did not see many students that looked like us. There were very few African American students present.

At the end of the tour, the student tour guide took us back to the admissions office where Miss Linda was waiting for us. She asked if we enjoyed the tour and if we had any questions. Roeiah and I had a couple questions that Linda eagerly answered. Linda also had a grab bag, additional information, and an application to the law school enclosed. We thanked her for setting up the tour and assisting us that day and assured her that we would be in contact. At that point, I still didn't know how I was going to get into Michigan State University College of Law. But then, it all began to unfold.

As soon as Roeiah and I walked out of the admissions office, a young, African American woman was approaching us. She had a big smile on her face and quickly introduced herself, "Hi, I'm Mary Ferguson. I'm the Director of Diversity Services at the College of Law. Are you all prospective students?" We told her that we had just ended a prospective student's tour with the admissions office. "I didn't know you were coming to the tour today. Do you have a few minutes to come to my office?" "Yes!" we exclaimed, quickly.

Mary welcomed us into her office and offered us a seat. She began explaining her role as the Director of Diversity Services at the Law School and her tenure in that position. "So, tell me about yourselves. Why do you want to go to Law School?" When Roeiah and I were done giving Mary our introductions, she had the biggest smile on her face. "What are your undergraduate GPA's and LSAT scores?" she asked.

Mary seemed to be quite impressed with both of our scores. We highlighted the fact that we also both had Master's degrees with high achieving graduate GPAs. Mary asked if we would mind if she called to see if one of the deans were available. She wanted to introduce us to him. She picked up her phone and spoke briefly to one of the deans, asking him to please come to her office to meet some prospective students.

Moments later a short, happy, African-American male came in the room and introduced himself as one of the deans at the law college. I was quite surprised, but happy to see another African-American male and a dean at that!

Dean Connell Alsup asked us a few questions about our journey and our desire to attend law school. Mary quickly chimed in and shared our academic accomplishments as well as portions of our story. Dean Alsup seemed immediately interested. Mary and Dean Alsup both said that we would make good candidates for the LEO Program, which was a program for students who needed an extra push prior to being admitted into the incoming Fall class.

Mary went in her drawer and gave both Roeiah and I an application for the LEO Program and asked us to complete them. Dean Alsup very enthusiastically explained the benefits of the LEO Program and how it could prepare us to start law school. It was somewhat of a jumpstart program for legal education. Dean Alsup and Mary both stated that they could not guarantee us admittance into the program, but they would try to advocate on our behalf. They explained that once you successfully completed the LEO Program, you would be offered a seat in the incoming class in the Fall. You basically had to prove that you could do the work as a regular admitted law school student. They both entreated us to stay in touch with them and they promised to keep us abreast of any developments.

On our ride home, Roeiah and I were ecstatic that we decided to go and grateful that we met Mary Ferguson coming out of the admissions office. We were extremely interested in the LEO Program, but understood that there would be some sacrifices that we would have to make if admitted into the program. If admitted, we would have to live on campus for six weeks and attend class four days a week. We would have homework and readings every night just like we were in a regular law school course. This meant we would be away from our families for several weeks.

Several weeks went by and I was on pins and needles waiting for confirmation of my acceptance into the LEO Program. I had researched information online about the LEO Program and read various blogs about conditional law school admission programs. It seemed like the perfect fit for me. One Saturday, I came home from the grocery store and there was an envelope from Michigan State University College of Law. I was too nervous to open it.

Finally, I sat down at my dining room table and opened the letter. It was my acceptance letter into the LEO Program at Michigan State University College of Law! I had to submit a $750 deposit within three days and prepare to move on campus within two weeks. *What in the world? My whole life is about to change!* I was so ecstatic! I called my mother, my grandfather, and a few of my friends and told them the good news about Roeiah and I being accepting into the LEO Program.

As I began to pack clothes and prepare to move on campus, I wondered what it was going to be like. I have never been away at school. Not even as a teenager or young adult. I was 30 years old at this time and had never lived on the campus of any school. I knew that I could come home on Fridays, but had to be back for class on Monday morning. I decided I would break up the monotony by coming home on the weekend and attending church services.

Saturday afternoon, my best friend, Joe, who is more like a brother, and I loaded up the car and made our way to I-96 Expressway to East Lansing, Michigan. It was time to begin my conditional admittance program into law school. My nerves were everywhere! Traffic on the expressway was stop and go. The closer we inched toward East Lansing, the expressway was like a parking lot. There were a lot of people headed to East Lansing as there was a game happening that Saturday as well as students were moving out of the dorms.

Finally, we arrived to the Shaw building where I was going to be residing for the next six weeks. We unloaded the car and I checked in and received my room assignment. Upon arrival to my dorm, I noticed the bunk bed and two desks in the room. The bathroom was the common area and was to be shared with the other student who was in the room on the other side of the bathroom. Fortunately for me, I did not have a roommate.

At five o'clock we had to attend a welcome reception for an introduction to our program. I walked into the Castle Board Room and saw 45 additional students plus their family members. We were all about to take on a new endeavor. I was nervous and scared, but determined to make the best of it so that I could be admitted into the Fall class.

There were ice breakers for students to get to know each other and a ton of information was distributed with our first homework assignment, which was due the next morning. Yes, the next morning, which was Sunday. I was totally surprised. This was going to be my new normal for a long time. During the reception they provided a light meal for the incoming students, family, and guests. After dinner, our family members left and we began to have exercises to get us acclimated into the LEO Program.

Sunday morning came and I ventured downstairs to have breakfast in the cafeteria at the dorm. I met up with

Roeiah and a few other students who we had met during the orientation. We all were excited and nervous at the same time. This was the beginning of the start of our law school adventure. During the LEO program we had to take Civil Procedure, Property, and Research and Writing classes. These were three actual law school courses, with actual professors, that we had to take with final exams at the end of the six weeks.

When we arrived at each class, we were given a syllabus, which had two dates and assignments. We had a reading assignment for each class with roughly 100 pages to read each night. My mind started racing, "What in the world? How are we gonna be able to do all this? How will I keep up?" I realized that this is what I wanted and that I had to do all of this and more to reach my goals. It seemed a bit overwhelming, but a professor came in and gave us some helpful tips on managing and organizing law school studies. This helped all of us to ease our anxiety a bit as we became acclimated to the law school process.

I will never forget Tuesday morning, only three days into the program, and I'm sitting in Civil Procedure and the professor calls on me to explain a court case that was in our readings the night before. This was the Socratic Method in law school that I had heard about. It could be so intimidating. After I summarized the case, the professor began giving me hypotheticals, with the fact patterns of the court case changing, asking what I would do. I was nervous, but was determined not to make myself look like a fool. I stood there shaking, almost sweating, but I survived it. I'm glad that I was one of the first as the professor went in alphabetical order. I knew that it would be a while before I had to do that again.

During week three, we had a quasi-midterm exam to see if we were understanding and grasping all of the material that we had covered thus far. I was a bit apprehensive as the new way of taking an exam had frightened me. I now had to use the IRAC method to answer my law school exams. That's the "Issue, Rule, Analysis, and Conclusion" structure to answer law school essay questions. This was a new way of learning and a new way of writing for me. With one of our midterms, in my Property class, I did extremely well, but I was having problems with Civil Procedure. I was struggling with the different forms of jurisdiction and standing in those jurisdictions.

I remember Dean Alsup encouraging me to reach out to him if I had any problems, questions, or concerns or needed any additional help. So that night I said, "Brian, this is only what you make of it. Get all the help that you can so you can successfully complete this program." I pulled my laptop out and sent Dean Alsup an email asking if I can meet with him. Surprisingly, he quickly responded and told me to meet him at his office at 7:30 a.m. the next day. I said to myself, "Seven-thirty the next morning? What in the world? I have class at 8:45 a.m.! I have to have breakfast and shower before class. Oh, well, there goes my sleep." I was going to have to get up an extra hour early.

I woke up the next morning an hour early, got dressed, and ran down to the cafeteria to grab something to eat. I quickly ate a bowl of oatmeal and a banana, then I walked over to the law college. The building was almost empty. No one was really there. I made my way to Dean Alsup's office and he was waiting for me. He was bright-eyed and bushytailed. *What in the world? This man is here waiting for me with a smile on his face.*

I explained to Dean Alsup my concerns and shared with him the results from my midterms. Dean Alsup carefully reviewed my results and began to ask me questions. Dean Alsup quickly identified the areas that I needed some assistance in. He commenced giving me different fact patterns and asking me how I would respond. It was a bit challenging, but I needed it to be successful. The dean explained that he would help me as long as I was willing to put the work and effort in. He told me to meet him three times a week at his office at seven-thirty in the morning to go over different assignments. That's right. Dean Alsup would give me additional assignments on top of what our professors were giving us. I had to do more work than my classmates.

One recommendation Dean Alsup gave me was to go visit my professors during the office hours. During this time, I could ask them questions and have them flush out any legal concepts that I was having a hard time grasping my mind around. "Boy, oh boy, here goes another requirement - an item on my schedule," I complained to myself. In any case, I was up for it because I wanted to be accepted in the program. So, every week, for the next three weeks I went to my professors' office hours and shared the areas that I was unclear about.

In their offices, the professors helped me to grasp the concepts and took time to explain them in different manners. One of my professors was greatly appreciative that I came to her office hours. *Why is she so appreciative that I came to her office hours?* I was so confused. She explained to me that of-tentimes students did not take advantage of professors' office hours to provide additional assistance and she was glad that I took the program seriously and sought out extra help.

No, it's not that I wasn't smart. It was the fact that this was new to me. It was a new concept. It was a new way of thinking and a new way of writing. I had to retrain my brain to think like a lawyer. Through all of this, I made it through the six weeks of this conditional program and it was time to take my final exams. I remember sitting on my bed one night sending out text messages to my family, friends, and church members asking them to pray for me, that I would do well on my final exams, and then be granted a seat in the incoming class. Everyone sent back prayers as well as encouraging words telling me how proud they were that I had made it as far as I had.

Even though I was working towards my dreams and goals, there were times that I really missed home. One of those moments came when I had to miss my brother, Justin's, graduation from high school. There's a thirteen-year difference between Justin and I so, in a sense, he was more like a son. I wanted to be there to cheer him on, but could not because of my obligations in the LEO Program. I made sure I called and congratulated Justin and told him how proud I was of him. I also promised that I would make it up to him once I was done with the program. In addition to that, I sorely missed sleeping in my own bed and home cooked meals.

When it was exam days, my nerves were shot and I could barely sleep, but it was time to perform. I woke up, got dressed, said my prayers, and made my way downstairs for something light to eat as I wanted to get over to the law college and sit in the library for a while and review my notes. After reviewing my notes for a while, I looked at my watch and realized it was time to get upstairs to take my first exam. It was my Property exam.

We took our exams just like we were going to take them in a real law school class with test proctors and all. The test proctors served as monitors and test administrators. Once the proctor handed out the exams we could begin. After reading the problem and fact pattern, I said to myself, "I can do this. This is the rules of perpetuity. I can answer this. This is simple." I began to chart out my answer in IRAC form, as well as, identify each component of my answer. I then took a moment to stop and think like a lawyer to say how I could counter this argument. Then, I countered the argument and went on to complete it. My nerves were all over the place, but I had done the best that I could. I had completed my Property exam. Now it was time to wait on the results.

Then, it was time for Civil Procedure. This was the subject that I had struggled in the most and was really concerned that I was going to fail. I read my exam and began to answer the questions. After about twenty minutes of writing I got stuck. I put my pencil down for second and quickly told myself to get it together. I realized my nerves were shot and anxiety was trying to get the best of me. I could not let that happen. I had come too far to fail.

I picked my pencil up and asked God to bring all things back to my remembrance. I began to answer the questions as best as I could and elaborate even more than what was required. Finally, it was over. My law school exams were over and I had to go to the dorm, pack up, and attend our end of the program event.

At the closing event, we heard closing remarks from our professors and the staff. They advised us what to expect after we left the University for the summer and when to expect to hear about our results. We began to say our goodbyes to each other and made sure we had each other's contact numbers. I packed my things up in my car and headed down I-96 towards home. During my ride, I was thinking to myself that I was glad the program was over and that I could finally breathe, but now the waiting game was about to begin.

Once I made it home and unpacked my car, I decided that I needed to take some time to celebrate my accomplishment. A few friends and I agreed to meet at one of our favorite restaurants for some food and catching up. Well, that turned into lots of food and laughs. Before we knew it, it was 10:00 p.m. and it was time for the restaurant to close. On my drive home, I heard a song on the radio with the lyrics, "There is nothing too hard for God." From the words of the song, I was encouraged to know that my acceptance into law school wasn't too hard for God. I went home believing that God was going to do it for me.

After a couple days of rest and sleeping in my own bed, I decided that I needed to venture out and purchase a couple of thank you cards to send to Dean Alsup and others who helped me get through the LEO Program. After all, I once heard someone say that people do not have to be nice and they don't have to be nice to you. Many of these people went above and beyond to ensure that I understood the lessons, concepts, and how to apply case law to each set of fact patterns. Even though I had already told them "thank you", writing a personal message was the least I could do. I went home and wrote personal notes on each card, addressed them, and mailed the cards off.

After a week or so I begin to receive calls from a few students who were in the program with me. Everyone was anxiously awaiting results. We all discussed some of the highlights of the program and how it helped change us and our thinking. It seemed like we were all nervous wrecks. Suddenly, I remembered something I learned in church: Faith and fear can't exist together. When I finished speaking with the others, I decided that I had to stop worrying.

One morning I decided that I would give Dean Alsup a call to make sure he received his card and to thank him again. I dialed the number, not expecting him to answer but, surprisingly, he answered. I told Dean Alsup that I just was calling to make sure he received my card and to thank him again for all of his help and assistance. Dean Alsup explained that it was his delight to assist students who had an interest in the law and those who took their studies seriously. He then let me know that the committee was actually meeting that day to make final decisions on admittance and that I should receive a decision shortly thereafter. Boy, did that put me back on pins and needles!

Just when I thought I had calmed myself, I was back being a worry wart. I started second-guessing myself and questioning if I had answered the exam questions correctly. *Was I prepared enough for class? Did I make a good enough impression on the professors?* All of these thoughts went through my head, but there was nothing I could do about it at that point, but wait. I resumed some of my normal activities like attending weekly church services, working, and hanging with some friends. I even went out of town for a weekend getaway.

A few more days passed and I hadn't heard anything so I called Roeiah to see if she had heard anything. She had not heard anything either and I began to grow a little concerned. We both encouraged each other saying that we would get through it and be successful. I ended the call with her and went on with my day.

The next day when my mail arrived, there was a large, white, thick, business size envelope in my mailbox. I immediately grabbed it and, shockingly, it was from Michigan State University College of Law. My heart began to pound and my hands began to shake as I wanted to know the results inside the envelope, but did not want to be disappointed. I took the envelope upstairs to my bedroom and sat on my bed and opened it.

I started reading the cover letter and it said, "Welcome to the 2007 Fall Incoming Class of Michigan State University College of Law." Tears began to fall down my face and I could not stop weeping. I had finally been accepted into law school. I was one step closer to my dream and this goal was a milestone. I had made it to where several people said I never would. No one, but God, could have done this! All odds were stacked against me, but my faith in God, hard work, determination, assistance of Dean Alsup, and others, and the prayers of my family and friends got me to this point. This was another testimony in my book that God keeps His promises.

I quickly began to tell my family and friends. In the letter, there was one requirement that I needed to fulfill in one week and that was a twelve hundred and fifty dollar seat deposit. *Where in the world am I going to get this from? Lord, I'm not going to be able to come up with all of this money!* As always, my mother and grandfather gave me the money that I was short to pay my deposit. I sent my deposit, along with the other required documents and, finally, I was an admitted student at Michigan State University College of Law.

D's Get Degrees

My seat deposit had been paid. I had read and reviewed all of the information that I had received as a newly admitted student. I was registered for classes and had printed each class syllabus. "Oh boy," I cringed, as anxiety started to set in again. It was time for me to get ready for a new student orientation.

A lot of things were going through my head. *How will I manage school, home, the commute to and from school, and family?* My grandfather had recently taken ill and needed additional assistance from my mother, brother, and I. Even though I had been provided a schedule of events for orientation, I could not help but wonder what I should expect at the new student orientation. It still seemed unreal that I was about to begin law school despite my past.

It was Saturday morning and I was headed to the law school campus to embark upon my new journey. The day was splendid, with warm weather, and the sun was shining brightly. My drive to campus was perfect. I listened to several CDs and had a couple of phone conversations on my drive up. After an hour or so, I arrived in East Lansing to begin my first law school challenge: service projects.

The service projects gave us a great opportunity to learn and understand that if you're going to be a part of the legal profession, you had to understand that the legal profession embodies an obligation to help local communities. This was a way to instill in us (the incoming law students) the drive to continue to participate in community service as part of our legal studies. This was easy for me because I loved serving and already had a life of service and giving back.

As I looked around, there had to be more than 250 volunteers from the Law College who provided much-needed community service to ten area nonprofits. Some of those nonprofits included the Boys & Girls Club of Lansing, Habitat for Humanity, and several others. We completed all of these projects while learning how the legal community helps local agencies make a difference in delivery of their important services. This was a great experience and the weather made it even more enjoyable.

There were several other highlights of the new student orientation, including a welcome session by the Law School Dean, a presentation on the *Introduction to the Legal System* by a professor at the law school, and a presentation by a professor on the law classroom experience. This was very enlightening as it shined a light on what I could expect in my classes. It provided a deeper look into the classroom experience beyond the opportunity I had during the LEO Program.

Another part of the orientation was visiting the student organizations and vendor tables, which were outside on the porch and lawn of the law school. There were so many student organizations present and the students manning the tables were extremely friendly, inviting, and willing to share information about their organization. I really learned a lot about the student body at the law school, but something didn't feel quite right.

Where are all of the black students? Are there any black professors? Are there any black staff members besides, Mary Ferguson? I saw several people who were in the LEO Program with me and we spoke with each other throughout the day. There were also vendors who provided resources for law students such as study aides, intern and externship opportunities, and more.

There were hundreds of students on campus (more than I had ever seen on Wayne State's campus) and parking was a serious problem. I went with a few students who decided to walk over to the bookstore instead of trying to find a parking spot nearby. It seemed like a short little walk, but turned out to be a long walk, especially in the sun. As we walked to the bookstore, we shared our thoughts on what we learned in the orientation and our musings on how law school was going to be. The consensus among all of us was that it was going to be hard and demanding. Everyone had a certain sense of nervousness in them.

As we arrived to the plaza where the bookstore was located, we could see a long line of people, standing around like someone was giving something away. The line for the bookstore extended out of the door. There seemed to be roughly thirty or so people in line in front of us. By the time we reached the bookstore I was hot and sweaty. We continued to chat while making conversation with those standing in the line with us. After all, they were our new classmates as well.

About twenty minutes later, I entered the bookstore with copies of my syllabuses and book list in hand. My first book was four hundred dollars. *What in the world?* I panicked a little, wondering how much all of my books would cost. After gathering all of my books, supplies, and study aides, I headed to the cashier. I couldn't believe what I was doing – I was really in line purchasing books for law school...expensive books. My total came to over two thousand dollars for my first semester of law school. "Wow!" I thought, "Not only is law school expensive, but the books are as well. Thank God for financial aid because I sure couldn't afford all of this." I kept telling myself that it was going to all pay off after a while. When the orientation activities were over, I went home to complete all of my reading assignments for the start of classes the following week.

A great deal of discipline and understanding was required to read all of the material and prepare for my classes. Between all of my classes, I had roughly 4,000 pages to read within a 4-day period. On top of that, I had to outline the cases that were included in the chapters of reading. I organized my schedule and to-do list to ensure that I completed all required tasks. I also tried to make time for some personal things like going to dinner, watching TV, and, most importantly, resting. I didn't want to burn myself out with this new schedule. When I completed each item on my list, I felt like a champion. *I can do this!* I was finally ready for the next day as a first-year law student.

On the first day of class I left extra early to begin my commute. I was nervous, excited, and I didn't want to be late and hung up in traffic. I had that kid-on-the-first-day-of-school feeling. As I walked into the law school, I saw students in the lobby, going in and out of the bookstore, and people just everywhere. This made me more skittish.

On the ceiling was a "Welcome Students" banner. On the walls were posters of a marathon runner and a quote that I first heard during the LEO Program from Dean Alsup, "Remember the marathon runner." This was a reminder to the students to take one day at a time, to condition ourselves, prepare ourselves, and remember to take small steps to get to the finish line just like the marathon runner. As long as I thought about the marathon runner, I was able to relax, but whenever my thoughts drifted, my nervousness sat back in.

As I entered my first classroom, I started to get even more edgy. There were at least one hundred students in the class and I started searching for a familiar face. I spotted out a couple of people who were in the LEO Program with me so I decided to sit near them. Moments later, the professor for *Civil Procedure* entered the room. This was a course I had taken in the LEO Program so I was hoping that some of the material covered would be a repeat.

Professor Filiatrault introduced himself and went through the syllabus. He advised us of his classroom rules and style of teaching. It seemed that it was going to be a very engaging learning experience. He started his lecture on the assigned chapter readings. I was worried that he was going to call on me to answer some questions about the reading. I survived the first class without being called on.

My second class was *Contracts*. The good thing about this class was that many of the students were in my first class so I sat with the same classmates. Our *Contracts* professor, Professor Mulligan, was new to MSU Law and it was his first semester teaching there. He set out his classroom expectations and briefly went over the syllabus. Then, he quickly dove into the first week's readings and lectures of contract law.

Some of the simple elements of a valid contract are the offer, acceptance, consideration, and no breach. That was one of the first lessons in contract law. We discussed many cases to determine when and how a valid contract was entered into. I wasn't as lucky in *Contracts* as I was in *Civil Procedure*. I was called upon to answer some fact patterns regarding contract law.

I stood up, shaking and panicky, but knew that I had read the material, outlined the cases, and utilized my study aids to better understand the lessons. Professor Mulligan asked me a question, which I quickly responded to because I knew the answer. But then, he presented a different set of fact patterns and asked me again how I would respond.

I had to stop and think about it and gather my thoughts. I wasn't quite ready for a different set of facts. I replied to him and he challenged me further. As soon as I would answer, Professor Mulligan would set out another set of fact patterns. Some I got correct and some I got wrong. I was glad the interrogation was over shortly. I sat down and my classmate, sitting next to me, said, "Good job." I was relieved. He had to make his way through the entire classroom before he got back to me. My day finally ended and I headed back to Detroit. On my drive home I couldn't help but thank God for all of the blessings He'd bestowed upon me. I was finally in law school and another step closer to my dream.

The next day I arrived to campus early to visit Dean Alsup. When I arrived to his office, I was shocked to see several students lined up waiting to see him also. I guess it wasn't so surprising. Dean Alsup had been a great help to me as I'm sure he was to those students also. I went to both of my classes and survived. My first week of classes was over and I had done better than I anticipated.

As the semester progressed, I began to get the hang of it. It wasn't easy though. The rigorous schedule had started to wear on me. I was still working part time and had a commute to school. I knew that I was going to get some much-needed rest over the weekend, but I also had to complete all of my reading assignments for my upcoming classes the following week. Over the weekend I spent some time returning some calls and giving updates to family and friends regarding my first week of class. This was important for me to do as many of my family and friends had been supportive of me and my law school journey.

Halfway into the semester, my classmates and I were looking forward to midterm exams. Surprisingly, in some law school classes, there are no midterm exams. The only exam you take is the final exam at the end of the semester. You have to remember and know all of the lessons you learned from the previous 13 weeks. This was why it was important to stay organized, take good notes, and have a system in place because there were no midterms! I decided that I would pay visits to my professors during their office hours to clear up any subject areas that I was unsure of and to ask some questions about studying and preparing for final exams.

During the semester I became very involved and engaged in the Black Law Students Association (BLSA). Through BLSA, I gained new friends with upper classmates who looked more like me. BLSA also had programs and activities to assist the black law students with study groups, exam prep, interviewing skills, and other resources during their law school time. One of the things that impressed me, while sitting in a meeting, was to learn of the many distinguished alumni who attended MSU Law, while at its current location and at its former location in Detroit.

Week after week, four days a week, I made my commute to law school. Finally, the semester was coming to an end. I had some good weeks and some bad weeks. There were times I fell behind on my reading, felt overwhelmed, and felt like quitting, but the winner in me said I had to keep going.

As I prepared for final exams, I was concerned about what grade I would receive. During our new student orientation, we were warned about not getting good grades, having a low GPA, and being placed on academic probation. I was so anxious because I did not want that to be me. I studied day and night. I attended study groups with some of my classmates to ensure that I had a grasp of the subject matters.

Thankfully, our professors provided review lessons to prepare us for the final exams. The review lessons let us know what possible subject matters were going to be on the exam. Another thing that caused my nerves to get on edge was that there was no traditional grading rubric in law school. The grading was on a class curve meaning, once the professor graded the exams, whoever had the highest number of points is where the A's started. The grading started from there on a downward scale and that's how the grades were allocated — with A, B, C, D, and F. So a student who scored extremely well could set the curve really high, but if you did "just okay," you could get a very low grade.

Two weeks later, I started my final exams and I was jumpy and a bit neurotic. I felt like I wasn't prepared, despite all of the studying I had done, but knew I had to remember the marathon runner. Luckily for me, I did not have two exams in the same day. During the exam time, the school culture was a little bit different. The hallways were quiet and the library was much fuller. I saw many students studying and countless others with somber looks on their faces.

One down, two down, three down... I was finally done with my law school exams. I was pleased, but then the waiting game for my grades began. We were told by each professor when we could expect our grades to be posted online. Whew! I was exhausted and sleep deprived. All I could think about was, sleep, sleep, and more sleep.

After checking on my grades for three days, my first grade had appeared. It was my *Civil Procedure* grade and I was shocked to have received a 'B-'. I was relieved and excited at the same time as I didn't think I did that well on the exam. "Where were the rest of my grades?" I pondered. I checked the next day to no avail.

The next day I received a text from my classmate, Jillian, asking me if I saw my *Civil Procedure* grade. I confirmed that I had. Jillian shared with me what she had received. We both were glad that was over and that we both had passed. We discussed our anxiety about waiting to see when our other grades were going to post. On the final day that all grades were due, I checked online and all my grades had come in. I looked at my grades and was happy until I saw a 'D' in *Contracts*. I could feel tears welling up in my eyes. I felt defeated at first, but then something inside me said, "At least I passed."

I called my friend, Judge Vonda Evans, and told her about my grades and expressed my discontent with my 'D' in *Contracts*. "Brian, D's get degrees! You passed!" she declared. We both laughed hysterically. I spoke with a few classmates who also had not done well in *Contracts*. However, one of my friends and classmates, Aliyah, got the book award. The book award was given to the student who got the top grade in that class. So, it was Aliyah that had set the classroom curve so high. I was glad that she received the book award as Aaliyah, Jillian, and I had started building a bond as classmates. Aliyah also shared that she spent most of her time studying for our contracts exam as she had taken a personal liking to contract law.

I decided to visit Professor Mulligan during his office hours the next week when we returned to class. When I looked at my overall GPA, I still was above the threshold for being placed on academic probation. That was a great relief despite the 'D'. When I arrived at the school, I immediately went to

Professor Mulligan's office and asked him if I could see my exam. He asked me what my exam number was, as no names are placed on exams. When professors grade exams, they grade them anonymously.

He looked through a pile of final exams and handed me my exam to review in the hallway right outside his office. I went through each question and reviewed my answers and the points allocated for each. At the top of the page there was a number circled in red ink. I went to Professor Mulligan's door and asked him if the number at the top of each page represented the total number of points that I had received for the questions on that page. I also asked if the number on the cover of my exam was my final point total. "Yes," Professor Mulligan confirmed, "Those are the final numbers for each page and the final number for the exam is on the cover."

I vigorously continued my review of the final exam along with my answers and the point allocation. I added up the points for each page. After going through at least fifteen pages of answers, I had added up each page and then added the total of all pages. I kept doing this and continued to come up with a number that was different than Professor Mulligan's on the cover. I added the numbers up three times and Professor Mulligan's number still came up ten points short from what I was getting.

I quickly ran back to Professor Mulligan's office and explained to him what I had discovered. Professor Mulligan quickly asked to see the exam. He pulled out a sticky note and began to add up all the points on it. When Professor Mulligan came up with the final number, he discovered that he had shorted me ten points. Suddenly, he began to shout some curse words, as he was disappointed that he did not add them up correctly. "How does this affect my grade?" Professor Mulligan looked at his grading sheet and said, "Well, Brian, you have just left the *D's* and gone on to the *C's.*"

I jumped out of my seat. I was ecstatic that I no longer had a 'D'. Professor Mulligan advised me that he would have to submit a grade change to the registrar's office. Since this was his first semester teaching at MSU Law, he was a little bit concerned how he would be viewed as a professor. I told him I was not mad and understood that mistakes happen and that I was glad that I came to his office hours to review my exam. If I had not, neither one of us would've ever known that I had a 'C' and not a 'D'. I couldn't wait to find to Jillian and Aliyah to share this news with them as we all were concerned about our grades. I wanted to encourage them to go to our professor's office hours and go over their exams as well. With news like this, I was ready to start my second semester.

My second and third years in law school were much easier for me. I had learned how to adjust to the law school demands and participate in other student activities. As the new semester started, it was also time to elect new officers in BLSA. Many of the former officers had graduated the prior year. Jillian, Aliyah, and I decided we would run for executive board positions. Thankfully, Jillian was elected president, I was elected vice president and Aliyah was elected treasurer. We came up with different activities and ideas to strengthen the black law school, especially how to incorporate the black alumni in our programming.

A bonus for me was that I eventually received a scholarship from the Sarah Franklin Scholarship Fund for the remainder of my law school studies. I was extremely appreciative for this as I was a struggling, juggling law student with a lot on my plate. My fuel expenses alone were high with commuting back and forth four days a week.

In addition to my classes, I enrolled in the *Plea and Sentencing Clinic* at the law school. Through this clinic, students provided appellate legal assistance to defendants who were incarcerated under the supervision of a licensed attorney. We were given different cases of currently incarcerated inmates who wanted their convictions appealed. We had to drive to where the defendant was incarcerated and, if it was too far, we had to set up a video chat with the prison. This was a great experience for me because I had already gone through the criminal justice process and it allowed me to utilize my own personal experience to assist incarcerated defendants.

If you recall, I mentioned that my grandfather took ill. Unfortunately, by this time, his condition had taken a turn for the worse and he was going to require more assistance. I'll talk more about that later, but, at this moment, I was at a crossroad as this would have added more to my plate. *Do I quit law school to take care of my grandfather? Or do I continue with school and come up with a plan to ensure my grandfather received the care that he needed?*

Well, I decided I was going to stay in law school. I had worked too hard to get there, but I had to come up with a plan so my mother, brother and I could make sure my grandfather got the care and attention that he deserved. It was a long process, but we figured it out. I moved my grandfather in with me. I just wanted him to get better and be around to see me graduate from law school.

Many days I went to school sleepless, irritable, and depressed. I had fallen into a state where I was just existing, trying to get through it as quickly and easily as possible. My whole life had turned upside down. I had a roundtrip commute of roughly three hours a day, several days a week. I was enrolled in law school, working two part-time jobs, and caring for my sick grandfather.

I had become overwhelmed and was extremely scared that my grades were going to be affected. I really did not know how I was going to maintain my GPA or even get a higher GPA with everything that I had going on. As time went by, I had to quit one of my part-time jobs and eventually quit the second. I was in a low place; a place I had never been before. I really had to lean and depend on God and tap in to my faith.

Times were so hard for me that often I went to school with a full stomach, having eaten breakfast at home, but with only a pack of oatmeal and or a sandwich in my bag to last me all day. Regardless of the state that I was in, I went to class every day with a smile on my face. Sometimes I had just enough gas in my tank to get to school and back home.

One day, I was in the library at school with Jillian and Aliyah and we were sharing everything that we were going through personally. Before I knew it, we were all in tears from sharing our different stories and experiences. We were all going through things that none of us knew that the others were going through. It was a significant moment and emotional release for us all. We sat there during that moment and all took deep breaths and afterwards laughed at how much it was needed.

Well, after three long years, it was finally time for me to graduate. I was extremely proud of myself. I had completed law school. This was surreal! I remember graduation day like it was yesterday. My grandfather was home, unfortunately, and in no condition to take the drive to East Lansing and attend my graduation. I put my cap and gown on and took pictures with him before my mother, Justin, Joe, and I left to head to my graduation. Our family friend, Barbara, agreed to stay with my grandfather while we were gone. On our way, we stopped by my Aunt Sally's and picked up my cousin, Brandi. Brandi was an undergraduate student at MSU and had an interest in law school as well. She later attended Wayne State Law and graduated from there.

When we arrived on campus, it seemed like people were everywhere. There were people moving from the parking structures in groups to the stadium where the graduation was being held. People were walking cheerfully with balloons, flowers, and other gifts in their hands. The excitement was at an all-time high.

As the graduates began to line up, I began to cry. All of my dreams and aspirations were coming to fruition. Jillian and Aliyah and I sat next to each other during graduation. As the ceremony was going on, I began to look around at all the graduates. There were only seven African American graduates — six females and one male — ME! Wow! God really did this for me.

The dean of the law school was going to be hooding each graduate, but because Dean Alsup had played such a tremendous role in my law school journey, I asked if he could have the honor of hooding me. As I walked across the stage and my name was called, I heard my family and friends cheering me on. My pastor at the time and my close friend, Judge Vonda Evans, were also in attendance with my family. Dean Alsup hooded me, gave me a handshake and a hug, and told me how proud he was of me. The feeling that I experienced on this day is still unexplainable. I just wished my grandfather could have been there in person to see his "Sam Bernstein" graduate from law school.

Even though I was graduating from law school, I knew my journey was not over. I still had to apply to the State Bar and address and disclose everything about my past. After a year or so, I decided that I wanted to go back to teaching and started as an adjunct professor at Baker College. I really enjoyed teaching criminal justice courses and sharing my personal life journey with the students. My next step was to pursue my Ph.D. in Law & Public Policy.

Even with all these accomplishments and times for celebration, I still had something weighing heavy on my mind and heart — my grandfather. He had suffered a stroke. He stayed in the hospital for several weeks and later had to go to rehab.

Keeping It Together

I had to alter my schedule to assist my mother as she took care of my grandfather. I would often purchase groceries and cook meals for them. At some point, my step-aunt, Kim, her husband, and her son needed a place to live. My mother agreed for her and Justin to go back to their old house and Kim and her family moved in with my grandfather. Boy was this a mistake!

After a series of illnesses, hospital stays, and health challenges with my grandfather, it was clear that my grandfather was not being cared for in the manner that he deserved. As time went on, my grandfather began to change. His appearance changed. He was losing weight. I discovered how true it was that he was not being cared for properly.

At that point I decided that I would pick my grandfather up every Friday and keep him for the weekend to ensure that he was nourished and paid attention to as well as to give Kim a break. I told Kim that I would pick up my grandfather every Friday at 4 p.m. after I left my part-time job. As the weeks went by, the time grew later that Kim would have my grandfather ready for me to pick him up.

The last straw was when Joe and I arrived at my grandfather's house and Kim said to me, "Make sure you get him something to eat because he hasn't eaten all day!" Kim was bathing my grandfather at a quarter after four in the afternoon. Tears began to form in my eyes as I could see my grandfather's physical condition was deteriorating. I stepped out of the bathroom and went into the kitchen to dry my eyes as tears flowed like clear, salty waterfalls. I couldn't bear to look at how my grandfather was being taken care of. I looked at Joe and said,

"This is the end of this!" Joe and I took my grandfather to my house where my mother was waiting for us.

After we got my grandfather settled in my house, I went to Boston Market, as he loved their meatloaf, mashed potatoes and corn. "I can't let my grandfather go out like this. I'll be damned if I stand by and watch him not be cared for!" I declared to my family. However, there was one thing that was pressing in my mind; I was in law school. What was I going to do?

I later called and had a conversation with my grandfather's sister, my great aunt, Sally. I explained to her what had been going on and told her that I wanted to call a family meeting. Aunt Sally agreed with me and told me to let her know when the meeting was going to be. Then, I called Uncle Alvin and my step-aunt, Jackie, and shared the same information with them and they both agreed. My other step-aunt, Toni, was still incarcerated in California so I wrote her a letter explaining some of the circumstances around her father and to let her know what I was looking to do.

At the meeting, I discussed all of the issues that were going on regarding Kim and her failure in taking proper care of my grandfather. Everyone seemed to be on the same page and was not pleased with the quality of care that my grandfather received. I made it known that I was going to have to step up and move my grandfather in with me as I did not like what I was seeing. I explained to my family members during the meeting that this had to be done in the correct and legal way.

I decided that we would file petitions in the probate court to take over the responsibility of my grandfather's well-being. I was going to petition the court to become his legal guardian and conservator. Everyone at the meeting was in agreement, but understood that, when Kim found out, there were going to be some issues because we all knew she was depending on my grandfather and his finances to take care of her and her family.

I wasn't concerned about what Kim was going to have to say. I was more concerned about my grandfather and his health. My mother and step-aunt, Jackie, completed both the petition for guardianship and the petition for conservatorship. They nominated me to be responsible for his affairs. All of my grandfather's children had to be made aware and the probate court sent notices to each one of them.

Needless to say, when Kim received her notification, she called my phone yelling and screaming and using several expletives. I told her I was not going to standby and listen to her talk to me in that manner. I argued that it was clear she could not handle the responsibilities of caring for my grandfather as she was not doing a good job and he needed to have better support. She cursed me out and told me she will see me in court and hung the phone up.

I immediately called Aunt Sally and told her what had taken place. Aunt Sally told me not to worry about it and that we were doing the right thing. She went on to say that Kim was going to have to answer for all of her behavior. When it was time for court, everyone stood in the court room while Kim was the only person objecting to me becoming my grandfather's guardian and conservator.

The court had appointed a "guardian ad litem", which was the individual to represent my grandfather's interest. The guardian ad litem had come to my house to visit and check on my grandfather and to ask him a few questions. Even though my grandfather's health was deteriorating, he still knew who he wanted to handle his business. With a clear mind and clear thought, my grandfather articulated to the guardian ad litem that he wanted his grandson, Brian, to handle all of his affairs. This was without any coaching.

The judge told Kim that he did not agree with anything she was saying and he was siding with the rest of her family and appointed me as the guardian and conservator over my grandfather's affairs. Kim began to tell the judge that I have felonies and had been in trouble with the law and did not need to take care of my grandfather's business.

The judge told her he was well aware of all that as I had already disclosed that, but the judge was impressed that I had gone and received both my bachelor's and master's degrees and was currently in law school. The judge explained to Kim that she could appeal his decision. She immediately went outside and drafted an appeal to the judge's decision. Throughout the whole probate court dealing, it appeared that Kim was high on some drugs and out of her mind.

After we returned to my house from the probate court, Uncle Alvin, Step-aunt Jackie, and myself went to my grandfather's credit union to take the court documents so that Kim's name could be removed from his account. Upon our arrival the manager told us that she had been waiting for someone to come and check on Mr. Banks's accounts. After speaking with the manager, and further review, we discover that thousands of dollars had been withdrawn from my grandfather's account and was spent at Motor City Casino! I was boiling mad! My grandfather never went to the casino. I thought, "How dare Kim and [her husband] Kevin steal from him!" We all stood in disbelief like zombies until Uncle Alvin began to use a few, choice curse

113

words. The manager told us that they saw a lot of that from time to time.

An ATM card was issued and all of the transactions were done with an ATM card. It was clear that my grandfather was not the person withdrawing the funds from his account. He had never had an ATM card in his life! He did not know how to use an ATM card nor an ATM machine and his driver's license had expired. Therefore, he could not even get to an ATM machine on his own! It was clear that Kim and Kevin had taken full reign over my grandfather's finances.

We had Kim's name removed from the account and waited on the final documentation from the probate court. The credit union manager told us she would put a freeze on my grandfather's account until she received the final court documents showing that I was the official permanent conservator. We were satisfied with her recommendations and I agreed to use my own personal money to take care of my grandfather until his situation was rectified. The manager asked us if we wanted to press charges against those who have taken the money out of my grandfather's account. We aptly responded that we would discuss it amongst ourselves and get back to her.

Once we began to get all of my grandfather's affairs in order, I discovered that the beneficiaries on his life insurance had been recently changed. I knew that my grandfather had not made those changes. He had suffered several strokes and dementia had begun to set in. After speaking with the insurance company, I had them change the beneficiaries back to what they were. It was clear that Kim had made those unauthorized changes. Once again showing her jealousy and envy of me and my mother.

The next order of business was to purchase my grandfather some new clothing and some new personal items. I scheduled a doctor's appointment the following week to get a checkup for him. When we arrived at the doctor's office, we learned that my grandfather had lost about 15 pounds. It was clear he was losing weight, but I did not realize it was a whole 15 pounds! My grandfather's doctor asked to see him back in one month. He also prescribed some medication to increase my grandfather's appetite. This was my new normal. I had to get organized and adapt to a new schedule while I continued to work part-time and attend law school.

My mother, Justin, and Joe developed a schedule and a plan to ensure things flowed smoothly in my house. By this time, Kim and Jackie stopped coming to see or even call to check on my grandfather. All of the work was on me, my mother, and my brother. It was no problem for us because my grandfather had provided so much for us. It was our reasonable service to ensure that we took care of him in the final days of his life.

By the time my grandfather went back for his follow up appointment he had gained 8 pounds and was looking better and better as the days went by. My grandfather was back to his old bossy, feisty self. After a few weeks it seemed that we had adapted well together and was getting my grandfather back on a healthier path. One of my daily prayers was that my grandfather lived long enough to see me graduate from law school. He was my biggest cheerleader and I wanted him to see me complete this goal.

As time went by, we developed a good system wherein I would prepare dinner in the morning before I left to go to school and my mother would come to my house before I left to bathe and prepare breakfast for my grandfather. She would spend the entire day with him, taking care of him, while I was away at school. Justin and Joe would help her throughout the day until I returned home from school.

After a while, my grandfather seemed to get the routine down and knew what time to expect me back home. I would often talk to him about how his day was and what I accomplished during the day while in school. Whenever I talked about being in law school my grandfather would always light up as my matriculation through higher education had been a long-time prayer of his. Truly God heard and honored his prayers (and mine).

I finally graduated from law school and my grandfather was alive to see that happen. I put on my cap and gown and took pictures with him to create the moment like he actually was there, but he didn't have the strength to make it. He was so happy and proud; he couldn't do anything but smile.

Sadly, after I graduated, my grandfather's memory and physical health began to worsen. One day while I was at work, my mother called to tell me that my grandfather had stopped breathing and that she had called 911. I told her that I was en route to the house. I ran to my car and broke every speed limit to get to the house to make sure my grandfather was okay. As I arrived on my street, I could see an emergency medical truck was in front of my house.

I approached the truck quickly and opened the back door where I could see my grandfather laying on a gurney. My mother was sitting in the front passenger seat. I began to ask the EMT if my grandfather was okay. Fortunately, he was still breathing. The tech told me to shut the door so they could take him to the hospital around the corner. Justin and I jumped in our cars and followed the emergency vehicle to the hospital.

I can't even describe what and how I was feeling during this time. My heart was racing and I was scared. I did not want to lose my grandfather. I knew he was tired, but I was yet selfish and wanting him to remain with us.

My mother, Justin, and I were placed in a family waiting room. Shortly afterwards, my cousin, Ingrid, arrived along with my friends Keith, Judge Vonda Evans and Judge Cylenthia LaToye Miller. We were all waiting and praying. I was expecting God to stabilize my grandfather and keep him here. After about an hour wait, the doctor came in the room and told us that my grandfather had ceased breathing shortly after he was brought in by the EMTs. The doctor emphasized that they performed CPR on my grandfather and brought him back, but he stopped breathing again shortly after and they could not revive him. As a result, they pronounced him dead.

What did I just hear? "Excuse me sir; repeat that? My grandfather is dead?" I listened in disbelief. I just could not accept it. I looked at my mother and she was an emotional wreck and when I saw my mother crying, I lost it. I began to cry profusely and ask "Why?" My friends tried to comfort me, but they really couldn't. I eventually landed on the floor, bawling. Cylenthia got down on the floor with me, hugged me, and allowed me grieve and sob. *Brian, get yourself together! You have to plan a funeral and make sure your grandfather gets the proper homegoing that he so rightfully deserves.*

Once we notified the rest of our family that my grandfather had died, it was time for us to begin making arrangements. Friends and family began to come by my house to pay their respects and offer their condolences. Many of them brought food, drinks, and cards and ate with us as we reminisced about the good times with my grandfather. One of the many sad things about my grandfather's death was that my Aunt Toni, who was incarcerated, was not allowed to attend my grandfather's funeral. This was all so unreal. The only father that I knew was gone. I no longer had my grandfather. I no longer had that one person who would do anything for me.

No matter how I angered him, he still was there. No matter how many times I used his credit cards without his permission, he was still there to support me. No matter how many times I told a lie, he still stood by my side. But he was no longer going to be there. *How am I going to make it? What am I going to do?* This was all going to be new for me. I knew I had to step up and be the man — the provider — for my mother and brother. It was at that moment I realized it was time for me to put into motion everything my grandfather taught me and everything we had planned together for my life.

As we prepared to lay my grandfather to rest, I thought about this as my final time for me to take care of him. I had to make sure everything was perfect. The casket, his suit, the flowers, and the program had to be just right for a man who so selflessly gave to me.

Once we arrived at the funeral home, my family and I picked out a shiny, black casket that would complement my grandfather's black suit, red tie, and the floral arrangements made with red roses. My friend Kyle, who is one of the best florists in town, designed seven different floral arrangements, including a casket spray, using over 500 red, long stem roses.

Joe and I returned to the funeral home a day or so later so Joe could give my grandfather one last haircut. Once Joe was done with his haircut, my grandfather simply looked like he was sleeping in the casket. He looked sharp with a fresh haircut and well-manicured hands. I was well pleased with how we laid my grandfather to rest.

Months after the funeral there was still one thing I had to do to bring closure to my grandfather's death and burial; I had to get a headstone for his grave. Unfortunately, when I went to have it installed it was too late, due to the cold weather. Ultimately, I picked out a headstone bench and, because my grandfather and Rose were buried next to each other, I even included Rose's name and memorial on the bench. After all, that's what my grandfather would have wanted.

BANK ON BANKS

I had become an adjunct professor at Baker College where I met a young man named Curtis. Curtis was a student in my *Criminal Law* course. He was very engaged, but a little withdrawn during certain topics and conversations. This one particular day in class, I had given out the instructions for a group project that was going to be due at the end of the semester. The students seemed excited and had many questions. I stayed after class to answer a few remaining students' questions. Curtis was waiting patiently.

After everyone was gone, Curtis approached me and said, "Mr. Banks, I really like this class, but I don't know if I will be able to do the group project." I inquired, "What is the problem?" Curtis confided in me that he was homeless and couldn't find housing due to his past criminal convictions. Curtis admitted that he was released from prison nine months prior to class starting for marijuana and heroin related charges.

He stated that he had served the last eight years in prison and, because of his record, he was being denied housing and employment. I advised him that I was aware of different programs and agencies that provided services to returning citizens. Most of them, Curtis explained, he had already inquired with. Curtis was a 52-year-old, African-American male who had decided that he needed to better himself with an education in hopes of obtaining gainful employment. *Boy, could I relate to this.* I began to share my own personal story with Curtis.

I described for Curtis all of my trials and tribulations, good times, and bad times. I shared with him that after going through the criminal justice system and paying my own debt to society, I truly believed that I had made some great strides with my life by continuing my education and receiving my Bachelor's, Master's, and law degrees, and engaging extensively in community service projects. I honestly thought that life for me would be a little bit different. However, I was gravely mistaken.

Many people like me, with criminal convictions, face roadblock after roadblock. We face an extremely daunting array of counterproductive, debilitating legal barriers that make it much more difficult for us to succeed in almost every important aspect of life. This was true for me, too, as I experienced denials for employment and housing just like Curtis.

All across America there is a lack of affordable housing and it is a never-ending problem for people who don't have adequate resources. Just imagine how much worse it is for people who have a criminal record. Employers adopt strict rules and guidelines for employment applications and often times deny applicants opportunities to interview because they have disclosed their criminal background. I personally went through this.

Despite having more than enough education and experience, I was denied some jobs because of my criminal history. I was very familiar with how Curtis felt because it had been too much for me. It seemed as if the rich were getting richer and the poor were getting poorer. I reached out to several organizations who provided services for ex-offenders or returning citizens. For me, the job opportunities were slim, as many of them were entry level and my experience and capabilities were much more advanced.

The semester ended and a new one began. I was glad to periodically see Curtis and other former students in the halls in between classes. Many of them would keep me abreast of what they were doing and how things were going. One day, I saw Curtis in the cafeteria and he shared with me that he had landed a job through a temp agency that paid a decent wage and that he would be made permanent after his 90-day probation period.

I told Curtis how proud I was of him and encouraged him, saying that things were only going to go up from there. He shared with me that he needed some assistance because he had to wear business casual attire. I quickly sized Curtis up and asked, "What are you...33-34 in the waist and a large shirt?" He laughed and asked, "How did you know?" He was about my size. I told Curtis that I would go through my closet and get him a couple of outfits. Curtis was shocked and very appreciative.

I asked him when he expected to be at the school again. He replied, "On Thursday." That was perfect because I taught another class on Thursday. Thursday came, I found Curtis, and the two of us went out to the parking lot. I gave him three bags of clothes consisting of shirts, ties, and pants. Many of them were brand new with the price tags still on them. Curtis became emotional and thanked me.

The reality was that I could relate to Curtis in many ways. I worked several part-time jobs from clerking at a law firm, to substitute teaching, to freelance legal writing for attorneys. I was appreciative of gainful employment, but I wanted more and I was growing tired of all of the turn downs and denials. After reaching out to several legislators and policy makers and getting no progress, I grew frustrated. I spoke with several friends about many of my issues. They tried to assist me also, and introduced me to different people in hopes of me ultimately obtaining more substantial employment, but it didn't happen right away. I wanted somebody to help me so it was my joy and privilege to help Curtis.

One day while on the phone with my friend, Judge Vonda Evans, I said, "I'm thinking about running for State Representative."

"What?" Vonda blurted out.

"State Representative," I repeated.

"I don't think you will go through with it completely."

"I've been looking into it and strongly considering it."

"...Go for it."

She was hesitant because she really didn't think I was that serious. A few days later while talking with Vonda, I asked her opinion of some campaign strategies and ideas. After all, Vonda was the queen of unorthodox campaigning. Vonda never met a stranger and would unintentionally campaign even when her elections were years away. Vonda probed, "You're really serious about this?" I replied, "Yes, I'm going to do it. I've prayed about it, talked with my family and close friends, and even spoke with my pastor about it." Vonda gave me her well wishes, but I could tell that she wasn't 100% sold that I was serious.

Nevertheless, I went on with gathering all the information I needed to run for office. Vonda later said, "If you're really going to run for State Representative, we need to come up with a catchy campaign slogan!" After going back and forth with several ideas, Vonda finally said, "I got it! Bank on Banks!" I repeated "Bank on Banks" and said, "Yes, that's it!"

In March 2012, I made my first bid for public office and ran for Michigan State Representative. I had worked on a number of campaigns and was even the deputy campaign manager for one so I knew a little bit about campaigning, but most importantly I cared about people and that would go a long way. I called a few family members and friends and hosted my first campaign meeting. Everyone was excited and ready to start assisting in any way they possibly could.

I sat down with a political consultant and went over everything that I was going to need for my campaign, including a budget. Now this was where I was going to have a problem. My budget was over $40,000. I didn't have that and I wasn't sure where was I going to get it from. I really didn't like asking for money as I was afraid that people would say no. I quickly learned that I had to ask if I wanted my campaign to be successful. My team and I came together and planned my campaign kick-off.

My kick-off was a great success with about 100 people in attendance. It quickly became time for the real work — Door knocking, mailing literature, phone banking, continued fundraising, endorsement requests, candidate screenings, community meetings, and attending religious services at different places of worship. This was going to take a lot and I was up for the task. I just had to address one big elephant in the room. *How was I going to put my story out and be accepted?* The district I was running in was very diverse. It included Grosse Pointe Woods, Grosse Pointe Shores, Harper Woods and a portion of the eastside of Detroit. The socio-economic status of the constituents in this district were all across the board.

I was born and raised on the eastside, right in this district, and every school that I attended from kindergarten to high school, was in this district. Furthermore, I taught third grade at a school in this district and many of my students lived nearby. I was sure that all of this would help me. I knew that this was going to take a great deal of organization as I was still teaching at the college and had begun my PhD studies as well. As time went on, my team and I had campaign literature designed and began knocking on doors in the district.

One of my favorite things about the campaign was meeting new people. I loved knocking on doors as I loved to talk to anyone I met. I loved sharing my personal story of overcoming challenges, my educational accomplishments, and what areas I wanted to work on to improve the quality of life for the people I wanted to represent. I also loved hearing the constituents' concerns and the issues that mattered most to them. Many of them were tired of the everyday common politician who only came around during election time. I had to reassure them that I was not that type of candidate. I explained that I grew up in the area and my family was still there. I went to school in the area and all of the issues that affected them had an affect on me, too.

Another thing about the campaign that I loved was attending community meetings. Community meetings are where neighbors gather to discuss issues that are plaguing their neighborhood, as well as, get updates from their elected officials. My mother would often attend community meetings with me. Her attending was a plus for me as she was born and raised on the eastside and knew a lot of people. People also thought that it was honorable that my mother would be out with me campaigning. I gained many votes and supporters because of my mother.

One campaign requirement, that was very time consuming, was completing candidate questionnaires. After completing and submitting the candidate surveys, some organizations wanted in-person candidate endorsement screenings. There were a total of five of us in the democratic primary and we were not only competing for the voters' support, but also organizational support and endorsements. I ended up receiving many of the labor endorsements, as well as, many of the constituency and advocacy groups' endorsements.

While out campaigning, I met many people from diverse backgrounds. I had many positive interactions. I met a woman in Grosse Pointe Woods who was an attorney. After sharing my personal story and overcoming odds, she asked if I would speak with her husband. She shared with me that he had become an alcoholic and gotten in trouble with the law for drinking and driving. She shared that he'd lost his job and ended up with criminal convictions. She thought that my story would give him some inspiration.

I also remember meeting a lady and her son in Grosse Pointe Woods who had a similar story. The son had gotten in trouble with stealing car tires and had spent ninety days in jail. The lady seemed to be really interested in my story. She encouraged her son, "Look at him! If he can turn his life around, you can." Talking to voters in Detroit was like talking to my family. I knew a lot of the voters and many of them knew me or knew of me through church, school, or my family. Along the way there were voters who shared with me that they would never vote for anyone who had criminal convictions. It was somewhat discouraging to hear, but I did not let that stop me from sharing my story.

With limited funds and a grassroots operation, my team and I were able to get my message across the district to the voters. It was the Friday before the Tuesday election and I was running around doing some last-minute things for Election Day. I had just ended a meeting with some of my Election Day volunteers. I was excited and anxious. All of our hard work was about to pay off.

When I got in my car, I looked at my phone and noticed that I had several missed calls and text messages. To my surprise, people were reaching out to tell me that someone mailed a "hit piece" out on me. They mailed a piece of campaign literature without saying who it was from. The mailer mentioned that I had felonies and asked the voters if they wanted a felon to represent them in the legislature. I was shocked and didn't know what to do. I immediately called a few friends and advisors inquiring what to do. After consulting with them I decided to send a robo-call out to the voters. Luckily, I had shared my story already with voters as my team and I were campaigning. They were not surprised.

At 6:30 a.m. on Election Day, my team and I were ready to head to the polling locations. We met and started our day with prayer. We thanked God for all of His blessings, for bringing us to that day, and for the victory that He was going to deliver when the voting polls closed. My mother and volunteers had prepared continental breakfast bags for each volunteer and ordered lunch and snacks for the entire day.

As I made my way to each polling location to greet voters and ask for their support, I saw many familiar faces. Many people that I met while knocking doors were at the polls and sharing that they were "Banking on Banks" and voting for me! "Bank on Banks" was really a good campaign slogan. Around 4:30 p.m. it began to rain and I thought that it would hinder voters from coming out to vote. Well, that didn't stop anything. People were at all the polling locations voting.

As I arrived at a polling location in Grosse Pointe Woods, a Caucasian lady approached me that I didn't recognize at first. She asked, "Do you remember me?" Right, when I was about to tell her "no," her son, who was parking the car, approached us, and I immediately remembered her. I said, "You have a new hairdo and a new color." We all laughed.

I remembered talking to her outside of her house. She divulged the issues that her own son had and his experiences with the criminal justice system. She looked at me in my eyes and said, "Mr. Banks, I normally vote Republican, but when you shared your story with me, you caused me to remember my own son and everything he had been through." She continued, "Your story was very inspiring and I appreciate everything that you have done with your life and everything that you stand for. We are on our way inside to vote and we are both voting for you." I was so happy and hugged both of them and thanked them.

As I made my way to the next polling location where my brother, Justin, was volunteering, those kind words of support brightened my mood. I had started feeling a little down and thinking that people were not going to vote for me. I started to wonder if my team and I had done enough to get my message out. When I approached Justin and asked him how things were going, he shared with me that the turnout was a little slow. He also shared that a lady saw his "Brian Banks for State Rep" T-Shirt and approached him and asked why she should vote for me with my criminal background.

Justin explained to the lady, "Yes, my brother has made some poor decisions and been in trouble with the law, but look at what he has done since then. He's gotten his Bachelor's, Master's, and law degrees. He's been a teacher and continues to give back to the community." Justin went on to tell her that everyone deserves second and third chances. The lady was appreciative of Justin and his candor and responded to him, "Tell your brother that I'm only voting for him because you sold him to me." I was so proud and appreciative of Justin because he isn't much of a talker and he used that chance to speak and support me.

As I drove off from Justin, I looked up to the sky and saw a big, bright rainbow hanging there. I began to smile as this was my reminder that God was with me and that it still was going to be a good day. By this time, it was 7:20 p.m. and the polls were closing at 8:00 p.m. I decided that I would go to a polling location in Detroit and end the night there. While at my last polling location, people were pulling up saying, "I came to vote for you."

I saw so many people I had met while campaigning. I even saw some of my former classmates from middle and high school. They told me that they had my back and told all of their family and friends to vote for me. At 8:00 p.m. the polls had officially closed and I had just finished my first election day as a candidate. I headed home where my mother and volunteers met up. We had dinner catered for everyone while we awaited the election results. We all were tired, but excited at the same time. Everyone was sharing their stories and experience of working a polling location on Election Day.

By 9:00 p.m., results started coming in. I was up six votes, then down three votes. I was up twenty votes, then down five votes. It seemed that Scott Benson and I were battling it out back and forth. By 11:00 p.m., I was leading by 30 votes with 89% of the polling locations reporting. Many of the volunteers had started to leave. Soon it was midnight and I was leading by 45 votes with 97% of the polling locations reporting. I was nervous and scared. I had worked so hard to get to this place. I didn't want to lose.

Unexpectedly, my friend, Judge Vonda Evans, called and told me to relax. She explained that she was at the department of elections monitoring the elections for one of her judicial colleagues and was monitoring my race. She told me that the absentee ballots for Detroit had not been counted yet. I was relieved, but still nervous. She told me that she would call me back when she had more information.

I decided that I would go take a shower while we waited. Once I was out of the shower and dressed, I returned to the living room where my family and a few friends were. I asked if there were any updates. No votes had come in. I sat down on the couch with my laptop and my mother handed me a plate of food and told me I needed to eat something. It was 2:00 a.m. and still no update. By this time, my friend, Roeiah, and her children stood up to head home. I walked them to the door and quickly took my seat back on the couch.

I hit F5 to refresh my computer and lo, and behold, I was up 89 votes with 99% of the votes reporting. My mother and Justin tried to hang with me as long as possible, but they grew weary and went home around 3:30 a.m. Once they left, I decided to go lay across my bed with my laptop in my hand. I continued to refresh my computer to see if the results had changed. Before I knew it, I had dozed off.

I was awakened at 5:50 a.m. by a church friend saying that she had just saw on the news that I won. I immediately grabbed my laptop and refreshed the screen and saw that I had won by 96 votes. I wanted to make sure so I check several media outlets for their results and confirmed that I had indeed won. I immediately called my mother and woke her up to the good news.

FROM LAW BREAKER TO LAW MAKER

On November 6, 2012, I was duly elected by the people of the 1st District to the Michigan State House of Representatives. Wow, what a feeling! I was really on my way to the State House. The district I represented was one of the most racially and economically diverse districts in the state. The day after the election, my cell phone rang nonstop with calls from other elected officials congratulating me, calls from lobbyists, and even lobbying firms with meeting requests. By the end of the day, I was exhausted. After all, I had been campaigning since March. I needed a few days to unplug and take it all in. However, I found myself having back-to-back meetings even before taking office.

As the days drew closer to the Opening Session Day for the House of Representatives, questions started surfacing whether or not the Republican-controlled legislature was going to actually seat me with my past felonies. Prior to running for office, I reviewed the State Constitution and spoke with other legislators, including one who had some criminal convictions of his own. Everyone confirmed what I knew from doing my own research: past convictions do not prevent someone from being seated and serving in the Michigan Legislature. However, since the Republican Party held the majority of the seats, it was up to them. They could literally decide to make my situation a political issue. They could decide not to seat me and I would have to go to court to sue.

Why would they do that? Would they really want to start the legislative session on those terms? Why would they want to make a scene on Opening Day when all 110 state rep-

resentatives are present with their family and friends? I honestly didn't think so. To get a sense of where the Republicans were, I arranged a meeting with the Speaker of the House. During the meeting, the Speaker advised me that he had no plans to not seat me. He stated that I had been duly elected by the people of my district and he was going to honor that. I thanked him and shared that I looked forward to working with him even though we were in two different parties.

Finally, it was Opening Day and time for me to be sworn in. My mother, Justin, my best friend, Joe, and another friend, Carl, joined me at the ceremony. Everyone was so excited. There were several opening day receptions prior to the ceremony at lobbying firms and in several legislators' offices that we attended. The atmosphere at the Capitol seemed to be quite jovial and there were no party politics at play. During the opening ceremony, all 110 State Representatives took an oath of office and were sworn into office. I truly could not believe that I had just been sworn into office. I really wished my grandfather would have been alive to see that day.

Once I was sworn in as State Representative, I was appointed to the Criminal Justice, Local Government and Military & Veteran Affairs Committees. In addition, I served as the Secretary to the Michigan Legislative Black Caucus. It was time to get to work. I had to set up my monthly coffee hours as well as my first community event. I met with my staff and we determined that I would hold standing monthly coffee hours every first and third Monday of the month. One of the coffee hours would be in the Grosse Pointe area and the other would be in the Detroit area. We quickly had our communications department design a flyer that we placed in businesses around my district, governmental offices, and mailed to constituents.

The first community event that I planned was for ex-offenders and returning citizens. While campaigning, I had shared my own personal story with the law and received a lot of feedback from those with similar stories along with stories of their family members who had been through the criminal justice system. I thought this was a good opportunity to have a panel discussion about returning citizens acclimating back into society while providing resources and opportunities for them, including jobs and educational services.

I had several attorneys, judges, probation officers, and returning citizen advocates on the panel. In addition, I had several lawyers present who could assist with expungements and address questions regarding getting convictions expunged. I was elated that over 300 people attended.

Every Tuesday, Wednesday, and Thursday I had to be in Lansing for session and committee meetings. Again, I was commuting back and forth from Detroit to Lansing. This reminded me of my days in law school. My routine became waking up at 5 a.m. and being out of the door by 7 a.m. so I could be in my office and or in committee meetings by 9 a.m. In between committee meetings, I often took meetings with other legislators, lobbyists, advocacy groups, and constituents who may have visited the Capitol. All of this was before session time across the street at the Capitol. Most days, around 4 or 5 p.m., I headed back home to my district. Many of those days I had community meetings in my district where I spoke to constituents and updated them on the work I was doing in Lansing.

My first month of coffee hours were a great success. My Grosse Pointe coffee hour yielded over thirty-five attendees and my Detroit coffee hour yielded over twenty-five attendees. People were eager and excited to hear and learn how state gov-

ernment was working for them. This also was a time for constituents to communicate their issues with state departments,
legislation and any other matters that were important to them.
Sometimes many of their concerns were not state issues, but my
staff and I always worked to help them get their concerns resolved.

One day while in my office, I received a call from my
colleague, Thomas (Tommy) Stallworth, who wanted to discuss
Michigan's current expungement law. He thought it would be
important to get my take and perspective as I had personal experience in this matter. We briefly met and Tommy quickly
looked at me and said, "Come with me... we're headed to a
meeting with Governor Rick Snyder. Several Black Caucus
members will be meeting with us to discuss expanding the expungement law."

Wow, just like that I was headed to my first meeting
with the governor. As I sat in the meeting with several of my
colleagues, the governor, and his staff, I looked around the
room and wondered if the governor and his staff were really
concerned about tackling this issue as it affected so many poor
and marginalized people.

During the conversation, my colleagues were making
the case that we needed to amend the law to allow for more
than one conviction to be expunged off of one's record in two
scenarios: 1) after a certain time had passed and 2) after other
steps had been taken by the offender. I began to probe about
expanding the laws to include conviction and offenses in the
same transaction. I had to explain in detail that oftentimes people don't go before a judge five and six times, but rather get
five or six charges, which lead to convictions, out of one transaction or arrest.

For example, you could get pulled over in your car for speeding and end up getting a charge for driving while your license was suspended, another charge for driving under the influence of alcohol and yet another charge for having a gun in the car, all at the same time. Then, you could end up having three or four convictions out of one transaction. This would automatically disqualify you from getting your criminal record expunged under the expungement law at that time. Then, the law only afforded a person relief of one felony conviction after they were released from probation for five years.

Many of the staff in the room and the governor did not realize that and began to ask questions around the issue. After much dialogue, it was decided that we would draft some legislation and activate some work groups to address the matter. As a result, the law was slightly changed to allow one felony and one misdemeanor to be expunged off of one's record after five years. This was not what we were hoping, but it was a little step in the right direction and would provide some relief to some Michigan citizens. I am proud to have been a part of that solution.

There were many controversial legislative issues that came up regularly. Some of the hot topics I witnessed included city emergency managers, public education reform, and auto no -fault insurance reform. With the Republicans being in control of the session agenda, it was important to stay on top of issues and be present because I never knew what laws they were going to try and pass. During my first term, I never missed a day at work and never missed a vote. It was important for me to be in attendance every day to ensure my voice was heard and to represent those who sent me to be their voice.

In addition, I thought it was very important for me to use my platform daily to bring resources back to my district and its voters to help provide a better quality of life. My office hosted events such as community health fairs, town halls, utility bill payment assistance days, education and job fairs, and an annual Christmas event entitled, *"Christmas with the Representative."* During this event, I adopted thirty to forty families and provided clothing, household items, food baskets, gift cards, and more to families in need. This was a great annual event, which included good gospel music from many notable gospel artists including Karen Clark Sheard, Vanessa Bell Armstrong, Kierra Sheard, Dorinda Clark-Cole, and many others who were not even from Detroit, including San Franklin, Kevin Terry & Predestined, Ziel, and Blanche McAllister.

Let me just say this about Blanche... I met her through a three-way telephone call, with a friend named San, over sixteen years ago. Blanche lives out of state and is a well-known gospel music recording artist. Blanche has a beautiful voice and has sung with some musical greats including Donald Lawrence, Walter and Edwin Hawkins, The Clark Sisters, Darwin Hobbs, Chaka Khan, Patti Labelle, and Stephanie Mills, just to name a few.

Blanche has trusted me to manage her as an artist since the start of our friendship. I have traveled the world with her and, as much as I love gospel music, it has been quite exciting to have her in my life. Blanche is so kind and understanding, but she will "boss up" when needed. I must admit, in my first year as State Representative, I indisputably needed her support.

As my first year came to an end, I reflected on what worked and what didn't work. I also had to take the time to celebrate that I had a 100% voting record and 100% attendance.

I never missed a day of work my first year. My staff and I had accomplished so much for our constituents despite some personal attacks on me from a news reporter and a former staffer. Wow, two years had gone by and it was time for re-election. Rumors had started to surface that I was going to have a primary election challenger. Well, that wasn't a surprise because most legislators who represented the City of Detroit always had a primary challenger. Term limits in Michigan made the elected seats more prone to challengers. As my re-election campaign started, I began to see my primary opponent at community meetings and different events.

My team and I remained professional and courteous despite my opponent running a dirty, mud-slinging campaign. My opponent and her team distributed material describing my past convictions and why they thought voters shouldn't re-elect me. Many voters shared with me that they were offended at some of the negative comments that my opponent was making. To be honest, it really bothered me that my past was continuing to come up. After all, I had moved on from it. *Look at everything I have accomplished!* Nonetheless, my team and I continued to share our message and the things that our office was able to achieve over our first term. Our message resonated with the voters and, in 2014, I was re-elected to the Michigan House of Representatives. Whew, another victory!

During my second term, I was appointed to the House Insurance & Appropriations Committee serving on the following subcommittees: Department of Human Services (Minority Vice Chair), Transportation (Minority Vice Chair), and Department of Education and Community Colleges. Additionally, I was elected by my colleagues to serve as the Chairman of the Detroit Caucus of the Michigan House of Representatives. This was the group of legislators who represented portions of the City of Detroit. This was going to be a challenge as there had not been much unity or togetherness with the Detroit Caucus for many years. However, I was up for the challenge as our constituents back home depended on it. Throughout my second term, I introduced many pieces of legislation to help Michigan residents address systemic and institutional racism and end oppressive and draconian laws.

As the Detroit Caucus started to meet monthly, our plates were full due to so many pressing issues plaguing the City of Detroit and its residents. The public schools were failing and there was not enough funding for the schools to remain open. Emergency Managers had taken over the city and schools and left them in much worse conditions than they found them. Auto insurance rates were at an all-time high in urban areas and, unfortunately, the list goes on and on.

More than ever, we needed each elected official in our caucus to come together for the betterment of our citizens. But the question was, how? *How are we going to do this with fifteen legislators who have different personalities, different work ethic, different logic, and different concerns?* Many of our caucus members rolled their sleeves up and began to work with me. We knew that many of our efforts were going to require resources to get our messaging out.

We planned our first caucus fundraiser and it was quite an event. Hundreds of Detroit's and Michigan's "Who's Who" packed in the Sohar Room at Sindbad's Restaurant and Marina. Throughout the room I greeted and connected with mayors, city council officials, county commissioners, company CEOs, lobbyists, grassroots organizations, and our loyal constituent supporters. Our caucus stood before our fundraiser attendees and laid out our legislative priorities and policy issues that we would act on. During the event we also heard from the mayor of Detroit, president of Detroit City Council and several other elected leaders. The overall event was a success as we raised money and met new friends and allies.

One of the main issues that my caucus and I had to face was how we get our residents lower insurance rates without taking away their consumer protections. The insurance companies in Michigan had been allowed to use non-driving factors like credit score, education level, occupation, zip code, and gender to determine what our insurance rates would be. This is called "redlining." This was clear institutional and legalized racism and discrimination. No one should have to pay higher car insurance premiums because they don't have a college degree or because of where they live or the fact that they are in an entry-level job. What does any of that have to do with driving? Unfortunately, this became a very contentious policy issue as the mayor and most caucus members were on different sides of the matter.

I worked day and night attempting to come up with a viable solution. I introduced legislation to end redlining in our state, which garnered bi-partisan support, but was never given a committee hearing as the Republicans who controlled the agendas did not want to take up the issue. It would require some of their constituents in affluent communities to possibly have to pay more for insurance. The mayor worked with the Republican legislature and introduced a bill for Detroit residents called D-Insurance. D-Insurance would not guarantee rate relief, but did take away protections for Detroit residents. Every media outlet was running stories regarding it and all the stakeholders (the insurance companies, rehabilitation providers, trial lawyers, post-acute providers) were sending their own messaging out.

After research, debates, committee and community hearings, our caucus, along with the entire Democratic Caucus of the House of Representatives, adamantly opposed the mayor's insurance plans. As you can imagine, this issue grew more and more contentious. I couldn't go anywhere without people asking about the legislation. I spent a great deal of time, energy, and effort educating the community on the matter. Needless to say, I and some of my caucus members gained some political enemies because we opposed the legislation that the mayor was pushing.

When it came to a vote, we were successful in defeating the legislation. I will never forget a Republican colleague, who was on our side of the issue, telling my colleague, Sherry Gay-Dagnogo, and I that we didn't realized how powerful we were. He explained that the talk around town was that we had defeated the mayor. He advised us to be careful as the mayor had a reputation of being a political pit-bull and being very vindictive.

Problems continued to grow in many of the urban communities such as Flint, Inkster, Benton Harbor, and Muskegon along with Detroit. Flint, Michigan, was in the middle of the Water Crisis, Benton Harbor, Inkster, Muskegon, and other cities were dealing with Emergency Managers controlling their schools and cities. Many schools in urban areas were continuing to fail our students.

I've always been an advocate for education and have been committed to ensuring that all children have access to the quality education they needed to reach their full potential and compete for good-paying jobs — no matter where they live.

Not to mention that there were many communities of color that did not have Democratic nor Black representation. Benton Harbor was the perfect example where the state legislators were White and Republican. Unfortunately, they were not concerned with the issues Black communities were facing.

It seemed as if no one cared about what was going on in the Black communities. I approached our Democratic leadership and advised them that I was going to start an Urban Policy Work group to identify and set policies and legislation to deal with these issues. I hosted several meetings and conference calls with key Black elected officials and stakeholders from across the state. We rolled out our Urban Policy Workgroup during a Press Conference where mayors, city council members, and other concerned citizens came to Lansing to support. This work was greatly needed. In the midst of this, I continued to be involved and engaged in my own district as my constituents were my primary concern.

In 2016, despite a challenging re-election, and some trumped up criminal charges, which I will describe later, I was re-elected to the Michigan House of Representatives for my third and final term. In January 2017, I was sworn-in for my third and final term in the legislature. My family was once again present at the Opening Ceremony and everyone was extremely happy. Sadly, our happiness didn't last long.

WHEN THE BOTTOM FALLS OUT

I had just gotten out of the shower and was getting dressed to start my day of campaigning when I heard a knock at the door. *Who could that be?* It was too early for my staff and campaign volunteers to arrive. I looked out of the window from my upstairs bedroom, but I could not see anyone. I went downstairs to the front door and no one was there. I then went to the side door and saw a white male and white female standing outside.

I opened the door and asked, "Can I help you?" The white gentleman asked, "Is Brian Banks available?" "I'm Brian Banks." The woman introduced herself as an agent with the FBI and the man was from the Attorney General's office. They asked if I had a few minutes to speak with them. I told them yes and I invited them in. I offered both of them a seat at my dining room table. I sat on the other side of the table, "Why are you at my house?" They explained that they wanted to speak to me regarding some "historical information." "Historical as an old?" They both confirmed, "Yes."

The female agent explained that they were at my house to discuss a loan that I had. I adamantly responded that I did not have any open loans at the time. They told me that they knew I didn't, but that it was an old loan. I shared that all my loans had been paid. They confirmed that they knew my previous loans were paid. The male agent spoke firmly.

"We would like to discuss some information surrounding one of your more recent loans."

"I don't know what you are referring to so I would need to speak to an attorney."

"You don't have to speak to an attorney; you're an attorney."

"I have a law degree and I, too, need to speak to an attorney."

They gave me their cards and asked me to have my attorney to contact them. *This was not the door knocking I had planned on today!*

Once I escorted them out, I proceeded to contact an attorney by the name of Ben Gonek. I shared with Ben that I needed to come speak with him because I had just had two visitors at my house. He advised me to come see him within the next hour. I confirmed that I would be there. After I hung up with him, I called Joe, who was at work, and told him what had just taken place and asked him to meet me at the lawyer's office at 11 a.m. This was a shock to me. It was so unexpected. I did not know what was going on. I had to figure out how I was going to lead my staff and volunteers throughout the day while I dealt with this matter.

At ten o'clock, my staff and volunteers began to arrive to start our week of campaigning. I called two staffers, Ron and Brian, upstairs to have a conversation with them. I advised them that I had had two visitors at my house and I needed to find out what the matter was regarding. I explained that I needed them to make sure campaign activities were managed for the day and ensure that all the volunteers received lunch. They both reassured me that they would manage everything and keep me updated. I was relieved because I knew I could depend on them to carry out the day's campaign duties.

After everyone had gone to start knocking doors, I proceeded to Ben Gonek's office. When I pulled up, Joe was already there waiting for me. We both exited our cars and I stood in the parking lot and explained to him exactly what took place. When we walked into Ben's office, the receptionist placed us in a conference room and told us that he would be right with us. I asked Joe to come for moral support and also to have someone else with me to hear and understand what was going on. As we waited, my mind continued to wonder what this was all about. I was in such a daze. My head was spinning with all of the possible things it could be and I needed to have someone with a clearer head close to me.

After a few moments, Ben came into the conference room. We greeted each other and the attorney inquired what took place. I described the series of events from earlier that morning and I also shared with him the business cards of the two officials who had arrived at my home that morning. When he looked at the business cards, he recognized the female agent's name and stated that he had worked with her in the past on the number of cases. He decided to call her to see if he could get more details.

While speaking with the agent, Ben explained, with a confident tone, that I had retained him as my attorney and needed some additional information. The agent went on to share the same things that she had told me. Ben told her that he would be in her building on tomorrow and asked if he could stop by her office to have a conversation and they agreed to meet the next day at 10 a.m.

Ben communicated the details of their conversation that we couldn't hear, conveyed what his next steps would be, and disclosed the cost of his retainer for representing me. We agreed to speak again the day after he had a conversation with the agent. Soon after, Joe and I left the conference room and headed back to the parking lot. I was completely numb as this was totally unexpected and I really did not understand what was going on. All my loans had been paid for several years and, as far as I was concerned, the matters were closed.

I checked in with my staff via phone and they advised me that they were sitting down having lunch with all the volunteers. They gave me the updates from the morning door knocking and explained that we had a very good day. I explained to them that I was headed home to complete some paperwork for the campaign and that I would see them when they finished knocking doors for the afternoon. I called my mother to let her know what was going on, but I avoided saying too much. I did not want her to begin to worry. My mother listened to me carefully and then said, "This has to be political."

When I hung up with my mother, I really did not know how I was supposed to feel. *What was going on? Who is behind this? Why would this come out all of a sudden? Yes, it was political season and, yes, people play political games, but would it stoop to this level?* These were all the questions I had in my mind. I had come so far and did not want this distraction. As the day ended, I spoke with my staff and heard that we received a lot of positive feedback and commitments from voters who promised to vote for me.

The next day I spoke with Ben and he shared with me that the Attorney General's office was going to be bringing charges against me for a loan that dated back to 2010. The loan had been paid back and it was almost six years old. Apparently, even though I paid the loan back, my income that was listed on my loan application did not add up. The argument was that the income was incorrect. *What was this about?* My attorney believed that something was really strange about this. *Who would go look at an old loan file?* He thought, agreeing with my mother, that it could be a political enemy.

What was even odder was the statute of limitations to bring charges against me was expiring in two days. This meant if charges were not brought against me in two days, they could not be brought against me ever. *How strategic? Why would someone wait until the last minute to bring charges against me if in fact they really thought I had done something wrong?* I was beginning to believe the theory that this was politically driven as the absentee ballots were being mailed out the very next day and most elections are won with those people who vote absentee. *Could this be a coincidence?* If so, it was perfect timing. It all just seemed so bizarre. I agreed to meet with Ben the next day along with some friends, advisers, and family members.

While in the meeting with my attorney, he explained that he was going to call to schedule a time for me to turn myself in to be arraigned on charges. Everyone in the meeting was shocked, but was not surprised that the Republican Attorney General at the time was doing this. Everyone had their own suspicions as to who was behind this as I had become a very strong voice in the Michigan Legislature and I had also been elected as the chairman of the Detroit caucus in the legislature. We had to discuss a strategy for getting my message out to the community. We planned a press conference and a rally for two days later. Everyone divided up the responsibilities as to who would contact who.

Later that evening the news broke that the Republican Attorney General's office was charging me with false information on a loan document. My phone commenced to ring nonstop and I began to receive a ton of Facebook messages and posts.

My whole entire world was being turned upside down. Even worse, it was being turned upside down while I was in the middle of my final re-election campaign to the State House of Representatives. Every news channel in the area begin to reach out to request an interview. I refused calls except for those few people in the media who I knew were my true friends and had my best interest at heart.

As expected, the news media was not only contacting me, but started to go by my house. I decided not to stay at home that night and stayed somewhere else to avoid all of the media. That night, my friends, Sherry Gay-Dagnogo and Judge Vonda Evans, came to check on me. They tried to make me laugh and take my mind off of what was going on. It was almost midnight and Sherry and Vonda were getting ready to leave, as I had to be up early in the morning to turn myself in. The very thought of this was embarrassing. I had a flashback of years ago when I went through this before. I didn't want people to think that this was something that I had just recently done.

As I laid in the bed I could hardly sleep as my mind kept going back-and-forth as to what really was going on. I was scared and nervous at the same time. I was worried about my mother as I knew she would be worrying about me. My alarm was set for 7:30 a.m., but I got up before my alarm clock went off and jumped in the shower. While in the shower my phone rang. It was my mother calling to check on me. I reassured her that I was okay and that we would get through this.

I met my attorney at the state police office where they took my picture and processed my fingerprints. It took all of fifteen minutes to go through the booking process. I then went to grab some food and meet a friend while I was waiting to be called into court to be arraigned. I met my attorney at the

District Court and there were at least three TV stations present with news cameras. In addition, the newspapers and a couple of radio journalists were in the court room.

All I could hear was cameras clicking, lights flashing, and the judge asking a series of questions. After being arraigned, Ben told me he would chat with me later as he was going to do some interviews with the news media. I proceeded home and, later that night, Ben called to check on me and explain the next steps. We also talked about the press conference and rally scheduled for the next day.

When I arrived to the church where my press conference and rally were being held, I was completely shocked to see over 250 people there. There were members from several union and labor organizations, churches, family, and friends. It was a bit of a relief, to see the diverse group of people standing with me during this time, and it was a blessing. Several people spoke in support of me at the rally. This level of support really helped me during one of the most difficult times of my life. I left the press conference and rally, not only feeling it, but knowing that I was not alone.

Later in the afternoon, my campaign team and I decided it was time to go back out and continue knocking doors and campaigning. I was a little bit nervous as I did not know what to expect nor did I understand what people were going to say. While some of the campaign volunteers were out knocking doors and talking to voters, I took the time to complete some candidate surveys and other things at home.

When my team arrived back at my house, I was totally shocked to learn that everyone had received positive feedback and words of support. We received more commitments from voters during that afternoon than we had on any other day. This really showed me that the voters in my district appreciated the work that I had done and understood that this was a political attack.

As time went on, one of my opponents in the race, continued to bash and bate my campaign volunteers. She wanted to cause a fight between the two campaigns. I told my team to remain focused and remember that we had a goal to win the election. Needless to say, Election Day came and the votes had been tallied. Around 11:30 p.m., I was announced the winner of the election. I garnered more votes during this election that I have ever gotten in any of my three elections. I was able to raise more money than I had raised during any of my previous campaigns, too.

Even though I had won my re-election, and felt somewhat vindicated, I was still going through the court proceedings fighting this issue with the old loan. Later, during the court proceedings, my attorney and I discovered that the wife of the assistant attorney general, who signed the warrant to charge me, had actually donated over $2,900 in support of my opponent and her bid against me. This contribution came in a couple weeks before the charges were announced against me. This looked like a political attack from several angles.

After going back-and-forth to court, I was finally offered a plea deal. The attorney general's office offered to drop the felony charges if I pleaded guilty to the misdemeanor and… I had to resign from office. *Resign from office?!* I quickly stated I would not do that because these charges did not have anything to do with me or my conduct while in office.

After talking to my family, Joe, and my friend, Sherry Gay-Dagnogo, I decided that I would resign. It was the consensus of everyone that was the best thing to do as I didn't have the financial resources to continue fighting. Plus, I did not want to be another black male in prison for a long period of time that did not equate to the crime. After all, I did not need a title to continue to serve the people.

I spoke with my attorney and advised him that I would take the plea offer as I did not want to continue to take my mother through this ordeal, nor did I want to continue allocating money for my defense. I reluctantly resigned and took the plea offer. I was sentenced to one day in jail, which was actually the day that I turned myself in to be fingerprinted. I didn't know what to expect after this. What was I going to do? What was I going to do with my life? I was ashamed, hurt, embarrassed, and so much more.

The day after I resigned, I woke up and I was mad as hell. No, I was as angry as a lion who was interrupted from eating a fresh meal! I could not believe that I had just walked away from a position that I had worked so hard for. I loved my job! I loved helping people. I loved creating laws to make people's lives better. As I stared out of my living room window, tears began to fall down my cheeks. I found myself becoming angry with God. I began to question God. *How could you let this happen to me? After all, I served and looked out for "the least of these."*

I checked my bank account and saw how much money I had in both my checking and savings. I said to myself "Well, Brian, looking at the money in your accounts you have five and a half months to figure out what's next." I had just enough money to pay my bills for the next five and a half months.

I did not know what my next move was going to be. I did not know what tomorrow was going to hold. I had just lost my lifeline really. What was I going to do? The bottom had just fallen out. The next two days were very rough for me. I cried and became even more angry and frustrated. I tried to encourage myself and say that it would be alright, but that didn't seem to help.

The next day, I received a call from one of my former colleagues and friend Tommy Stallworth. Tommy called to check on me and to discuss what my next move was going to be. I told him I really didn't know, but was going to take some time to think and pray. Tommy told me I should consider starting a consulting company. He told me that I knew the legislative issues and that I had built some great relationships at the capital and in the community. He shared that he thought I would make a great advocate and consultant for many people and their organizations.

I didn't know what to make of that since I never considered working for myself and I wasn't confident in whether or not anyone would hire me to be their consultant. After all, I had just resigned from office. Nonetheless, I called a few friends in the lobbying and consulting business and ran the idea by them. All of them were very supportive and told me that I should explore it.

I reached out to an attorney I knew that could help me establish my consulting company. I explained to her what I wanted to do and she told me she would take care of everything. She asked me several questions about business structure and plans. I told her the name that I wanted my company to be called and she agreed to take it from there. A couple of days later she called to let me know that all of my paperwork had been filed and that I was officially a small business owner.

Wow! I could hardly believe it. I was about to become a business owner. I reached out to a couple of friends, Kevin and Devin, to update them on my plans and to get some insight. Kevin and Devin shared with me that they had discussed an idea involving me being a consultant and wondered if I would be interested. A few days later they advised me that they wanted me to provide them a proposal for consulting work. I quickly put together a proposal and sent it off. Surprisingly, they accepted my proposal and sent my signed proposal back with the requested retainer. Before I knew it, God continued to bless me with client after client after client!

Within weeks, my telephone began to ring and I began to receive Facebook messages from people asking for my support with their candidacy to replace me as State Representative. Most of the people I really didn't have a relationship with. I wanted to ensure that whoever followed me as a state representative in my district cared for the constituents as I did, that they would vote with the people's best interest, and look after the seniors and children in the district.

My younger brother, Justin, had considered it for a while, but later decided against it. I reached out to my childhood friend, Tenisha, and asked her to think about it. I shared with her that I would support her and be with her every step of the way. Tenisha and I grew up on the same street and went to elementary and high school together. We were currently living two blocks away from each other.

Tenisha finally decided to take me up on my offer and run for state representative. We assembled a campaign team and campaigned almost every day to make sure that the voters knew who Tenisha was. Many days Tenisha and I campaigned together which gave me the opportunity to let the voters know that I was supporting Tenisha and I wanted them to consider her. After several months of campaigning, Tenisha won and became my successor. Our hard work had finally paid off and, with a good friend like Tenisha, I believed the people I cared for were in good hands. Unfortunately, everybody that had come in my life were not good friends.

FRIENDS, HOW MANY OF US HAVE THEM?

I've fallen out with people that I never thought I would. When you are betrayed by people you trusted with all of your heart it hurts. I was used by people I would do anything for. My relationships have also had a beautiful side though. I have been loved by someone I never thought would have loved me. I've formed new friendships with people whom I now have a more meaningful and stronger camaraderie. I needed them all to overcome some things I never thought I would get over. We all have chapters that end with people out of them, at some point in life, but I take pride in knowing that the very best part of my book is still being written.

As long as I can remember, I've heard the saying, "Some people come into your life for a reason, season, or a lifetime." The lesson I've learned is that it is up to me to determine in which category people fall. From a child I was quick to say "he's my friend" or "she's my friend", but that was not always the case. As I look over my life, I believe I used the word "friend" too freely. Yes, the bible says ... "there is a friend that sticketh closer than a brother," but the bible also talks about the kind of friend who betrays you, lies on you, and simply lets you down. Some of my friendships were life-changing and, at different phases of my life, I had people who I will forever remember.

If you have a cousin, then you know that cousins can be your first friends and my first friends were Anthony and Kelvin. Anthony is my Step-aunt Jackie's son. Anthony and

Jackie were often at our house when we lived with my grandfather, therefore, Anthony and I often played together. Even though we were cousins, there always seemed to be some form of tension between us. I guess that was a result of Anthony's learned behavior from his mother and her deep-rooted dislike for my mother and I and our relationship with my grandfather.

As Anthony and I got older our relationship grew further and further apart. To this day we don't see each other often. Honestly, I still feel some kind of way with Anthony for not attending our grandfather's funeral. After all, our grandfather was a father to both of us at young ages especially since neither one of our fathers were in our lives. I eventually had to let go of those feelings as it was not doing anything positive for me.

Kelvin is my Great Aunt Sally's youngest son. My mother and I went to my Aunt Sally's house often, especially to escape the madness at home with Rose, Kim, and Jackie. Kelvin and I often played together. Kelvin took up barbering and cosmetology after my Aunt Sally and would often practice on my hair; several times he left bald patches in my head that Aunt Sally would have to fix. My mother often took Kelvin and I downtown, by public transportation, to go to the movies and enjoy food at an old restaurant called *Flaming Embers*. I looked forward to riding the bus and observing the many people who rode along with us. As adults, Kelvin and I often talk and see each other.

Even though Anthony and Kelvin both are my cousins, Kelvin and I share the same ideas when it comes to family. Kelvin and I both believe that family is everything and that you should support each other — no matter what. Anthony, on the other hand, is okay, and has been okay, with not being in communication with his family. My relationship with Anthony has taught me that even though you may be blood relatives, and may have even been raised together, those things don't equate to having a solid relationship as adults and sometimes you are closer to some family members than others.

One of my elementary school friends was Tenisha. Tenisha and I lived on the same street and went to elementary and high school together. Tenisha and I would often get in trouble for talking in class and would often talk on the phone in the evening after school. There was a short period after high school where Tenisha and I didn't see or connect with each other. When we did run back into each other for a while, we picked up like there was no break in our communication. Later in life as adults, we both somehow ended up living downtown in the same complex.

As a young adult, Tenisha ended up having some troubles of her own which caused her to spend a month or two in jail. Luckily, we both got our stuff together and Tenisha graduated and received her bachelor's and law degrees. She then became an assistant prosecuting attorney even with felonies and misdemeanors. Currently, we live one street over from each other and regularly discuss legislative and policy issues, community concerns or just to catch up. This is the same Tenisha who succeeded me after I resigned from office. This shows that some friendships will last a lifetime even if you have moments where you don't see, or communicate with, each other. Some friendships were built to last and this one, with Tenisha, is definitely one of them.

During my young adult years, I attended a new church and started to gain and develop new friendships. This included Jonathan, Vincent, Angela, and Beverly. All of them had different places in my life. Jonathan was the choir president and lived two streets over. Jonathan knew several of my family members as he went to school with them and even went to cosmetology school with a couple of them. Jonathan was older than me, but we both enjoyed church, gospel music, and traveling. Through Jonathan, I met Vincent.

Vincent, at the time we met, attended another church. It was ironic, and a small world, as Vincent would come to my house for him and his girlfriend to get their hair done by my Step-aunt Kim. Jonathan, Vincent, and I often took road trips, hung out at each other's homes, and attended parties together. As a young adult, I had some good times hanging with these two. Even though we don't see each other often, I still connect with both Jonathan and Vincent occasionally. Life may have taken us down different paths, but, Jonathan, Vincent, and I have a genuine love and respect for each other and each other's families.

Church is a good place to meet friends, as you can see. I don't know what I would have done without the solace and consistency of my church friends like Angela, but there were others, like Beverly, who were a whole other story. I met Angela (Angie) and Beverly through singing with a community choir. Angie and Beverly had known each other from years back. As a choir, we traveled around the city, singing at different churches and engagements and, over time, our friendships grew closer. Angie loved music, like me, and developed a style of her own. Angie, a single mother who currently lives in Chicago, raised a smart young man, and is more like a sister to me. To this day, Angie and I are very supportive of each other and talk frequently even though we live in two different states.

Now, Beverly and I became really close and developed what I thought was a brother/sister bond. We were so close that I helped her buy diapers and baby formula for her son when he was a baby. I helped with her telephone and utility bills, loaned money, paid for trips, hair appointments, gas — you name it and I did it. All this took place while Beverly was married. Beverly's marriage had some interesting times, which often left Beverly and her son without. As a friend and brother, I stepped up to help often times putting their needs before mine.

There were secrets that I kept from her other friends and family, as well as, things that she has done that would totally embarrass her family and friends. You would think that would keep us in a good place, right? Well, the Beverly that I once knew changed. She betrayed me, lied on me, and even set me up to die without even having any remorse or consideration for my mother and the rest of my family. I could go on further about this person, but why waste the energy? Needless to say, our friendship is no more and I live as if she does not exist. Even this situation had to happen, but it wasn't the easiest lesson to learn that you cannot even allow the deepest hurt and pain change your character and keep you away from pursuing your dreams.

Now these next two friends are known throughout the Detroit church community. Keith and Carl have been around for literally ages. What's funny is that I met both of them at different times and found out that they were close friends. Keith and I met through a mutual friend, Kyle, at one of Kyle's birthday parties. At the time, Keith was much heavier and loved to eat. That was a plus in my book because I loved to eat as well! You could often find Keith and I at different restaurants trying out new things. Keith and I have been there for each other during some of the darkest hours in our lives including Keith losing his mother and me losing my grandmother and grandfather.

Keith and I ended up being members of the same church for a while and we spent even more time together, but he eventually left and joined another church. Now, don't get me wrong, there have been numerous times where Keith has done something or has said something that I didn't like or didn't agree with. Even though we had our disagreements, we still check in with each other from time to time.

While I was working at United Airlines, I met Carl. Carl also lived on the eastside and we had a lot of friends in common, therefore, we ran into each other often. From time to time, Carl and I, with a group of friends, would get together to dine out or enjoy fellowship at someone's house. Years later, Carl and his parents ended up being my neighbors. This allowed us to get to know each other very well.

Carl and I are members of the same church and still communicate frequently. Carl and I can take a break from each other and pick up like nothing ever happened. My friendships with Keith and Carl had to happen to teach me that, even in true friendships, there have to be some boundaries set in order to respect each other and respect each other's different opinions. These boundaries could simply mean learning what to share, with who, and when to share.

Of course, there is my friend, Joe, who I met before going to law school. Joe has truly become a family member to me. He's just the kind of person who is with you through thick and thin consistently. I have shared my most exciting moments with him, like the day I rode up to Michigan State for the LEO Program, and also my most devastating moments, like the day my grandfather passed.

As the years have gone by, I have learned to accept Joe and his mean, Gemini ways! I just decided to deal with it, as I'm sure he has had to decide to deal with me with my Scorpio ways. Joe has helped me with so many things in life – getting through school, going through several court experiences, and legal encounters — and he has been a constant listening ear. A fifteen-year friendship has developed into a brotherly bond that just cannot be broken.

I love people who have a genuine love for mankind and helping others. It seems that these individuals are some of the people who I gel with the most. It is an added plus for me if you are in the business of helping people change their lives for the better. The next set of friends I want to tell you about exude love for mankind, are committed to reaching back, giving to others, and seeing the good in everyone.

Retired Judge Vonda Evans and I became friends almost sixteen years ago. Vonda and I met through a mutual attorney friend one summer while hanging out in downtown Detroit. Anyone who knows Vonda, knows that everything has to be Vonda's way! I think it's an only child thing, and I'm laughing now as I think about it, but we've remained friends in spite of it. Many people don't understand Vonda, but I understand her and therefore govern myself accordingly. She is the life of the party and I love her dearly (even when I need to take a break from her)!

Let's hear it for the Honorable Sherry Gay-Dagnogo, State Representative for Michigan's 8th House District! Sherry and I have been friends for over twenty-four years through church. We have several mutual friends also. Later in life, Sherry and I ran for the State House during the same year. Unfortunately, Sherry didn't win that election, but later joined me in office two years later.

Sherry is a very strong woman with a good heart. We both have such strong church backgrounds and lean heavily on our faith. Many folks don't understand us and our relationship, but we speak frequently as we're two of a kind. When we love, we love hard. No one would ever know if we had a disagreement because whenever we do not agree, we align on a matter before we're in front of others. I marvel at how we consistently make that work.

What can I say about my dear friend, Judge Cylenthia LaToye Miller? Yes, you have to say her entire name – Cylenthia LaToye Miller! She was a mentor for me while I was in law school and eventually became like family. We've watched each other grow and take prominent roles in the political world. From a district court judge to now a circuit court judge, I've been with her every step of the way. We've both seen some hard times with our families, but my big sister, Cylenthia, and I survived.

Vonda, Sherry, and Cylenthia all represent people who genuinely care about others. They're not just friends, but they are phenomenal leaders. They're well educated, experienced, and respected African American women. They all have served others respectfully and have helped change people's lives in some way or another just like I want to positively impact others. These friendships had to happen to remind me that regardless of how successful you are, you must never forget to reach back and help others.

Now there's something about the DMV area and me. I have established some of the best friendships in the DMV. Let's talk about my BFF, Ebony (Eb). Ebony and I met through a mutual acquaintance whom neither of us speak with to this day. How funny is that? We hit it off right from the start. Ebony resides in Maryland and loves, loves sports. She has worked for several major league sporting teams. For a year, Ebony had to opportunity to move to Detroit and stay with me when she first moved. This allowed our bond to get even closer.

Ebony and I have confided in each other and have never minced words nor had a falling out. Ebony is a whole mood by herself. Ebony is that one friend that everyone loves and can say something good about. She is loyal to a fault, which is one of the reasons I love me some Eb. Ebony and I are very supportive of each other and our initiatives. I've learned with Ebony that the length of time that you've known someone doesn't matter as much as the magnitude of the friendship.

During one of my many visits to D.C. I had dinner with Ebony and a friend from Detroit, who now resides in the DMV, who brought along a gentleman named Terrence. From there, Terrence and I gelled and have been brothers ever since. We learned quickly that we had so much in common. Being from Chicago, Terrence and I both have a love for the Midwest. He also has a love for politics and mankind. These shared interests keep our connection strong and we always find ways to support each other despite our physical distance. Even though we're not in a fraternity together, Terrence and I have built our own strong brotherhood.

My journey to law school was tumultuous and I could not have done it without my closest law school friend, Jillian. We took almost every class together, spent summers together, and shared in the joys of graduation. Jillian has remained a true friend, beyond graduation, even if it takes her 40,000 days to return a call! Jillian and her family have supported all of my endeavors and I am forever indebted to them.

My friendships with Ebony, Jillian, Terrence and another DMV friend, Gerald, all mean the world to me and they all have taught me that some of your closest friendships will be distances away. Often times it's not the people you spend the most time with who you are the closest with. These friendships had to happen to teach me and show me that love and true friendships know no distance.

Even through work and professional affiliations, I've been able to develop friendships. When I first took office in 2013, Tommy Stallworth really took me under his wing as a young, elected legislator and showed me the ropes. Tommy invited me into meetings that I knew nothing about and exposed me to the governor, high ranking officials, community leaders, and other elected officials. Tommy kept me involved and engaged.

Now Tommy is somewhat older than me so, I revered him as my "legislative father." Tommy helped me obtain support for amendments and bills, got them passed, and prepared me to be the next chairman of the Detroit Caucus. I have a great deal of respect for Tommy and, even when we didn't see eye-to-eye on legislation and candidates for political races, our friendship remained unshakable.

While I was in office, I worked with two gentlemen on several important legislative issues. Devin and Kevin are in a league all by themselves. When I resigned from office both Devin and Kevin remained in my corner and was extremely supportive of my next steps. Let me be very clear... these two believed in me and supported me when I wanted to give up. They made sure I ate and that I ate well! They entrusted me to represent them and their organizations as their consultant (for three years now) and, for that, I am forever indebted.

My friendships with Tommy, Devin, and Kevin had to happen so I would understand that even in professional relationships, meaningful friendships can develop and you need them. Sometimes the best camaraderie is with people who don't necessarily look like you or who may not have had the same life experiences as you. I hope you can see that I've learned how to embrace all kinds of people; some were older, others from different parts of the country, and yet others from different religious or ethnic backgrounds.

Regardless to where life has taken you and your friends, real friends are present during times of importance. As an adult, I've made a conscious effort to be more supportive of and "present" for my friends. Sometimes it can be an inconvenience, but it's worth it. At some point you have to learn who (and what) is really important. Last year, I was happy that over twenty-five of my friends flew to Florida and spent my birthday weekend with me in sunny Ft. Lauderdale and Miami, Florida.

While I have other companions and acquaintances, I wanted to highlight these individuals because they have been pivotal in my life. I've learned to respect them and learn from them. With each new person came a different character and personality. Each of them had different needs and expectations of me. I had to learn to open up with them and how to set boundaries.

In life, it's important to have family and friends in your corner. There will be some friends that will stick and stay with you, while others will hang around only when it's convenient. I've found that it's important to identify those "convenient friends" early. I personally experienced people that I had been there for, supported, loaned money, been a listening ear, and more, who did not reciprocate that same level of support. I discovered when things were going well they were some of the loudest cheerleaders. Conversely, when times became tough for me, some of those friends would disappear.

I'm sure you've experienced the reality that some people are just flat out users and opportunists. Some people are only around when it benefits them. It's sad, but it's true. There are self-serving people out here. They key to life is not being one of them because, if you are, you will be discovered, too. There is a lesson for you even when friendships end or don't go the way that you think they should go. Don't beat up on yourself. Learn the lesson and keep going. Each relationship I described, even those that went sour, had to happen to get me to where I am today and, for that, I am truly grateful.

IF I HAD KNOWN IN THE
BEGINNING...

It was a very cold, Sunday morning in Nashville, Tennessee. The air was very calm and dry. I was in the city for the Stellar Gospel Music Awards, which were held on the previous night. I had about three hours to spare before my two-hour flight back home to Detroit, Michigan. So, I decided to grab a bite to eat, take a walk through the mall, and see what I could find. I found a sweater and scarf that seemed to suit me so I purchased them and headed toward my gate.

On the flight home to Detroit, I remember feeling revived and excited about the week's events, especially the meeting about my book and beginning the process of becoming a published author. The next day was the Monday that we celebrate the birthday and dream of Dr. Martin Luther King, Jr. On the plane I began to reflect on my schedule for the following day.

Time	Event	Purpose
8:30-9:30 AM	Coffee Hours	Meeting with constituents at McDonald's to provide them with legislative updates
10:30 AM	Lobbyists' Meeting	Meeting with several lobbyists to discuss policy issues and legislation
12:15 PM	Interview with Book Consultant	Introductory interview for producing my 1st Novel/ Autobiography
2:15 PM	1:1 Appointment	Potential Candidate for State Senate
6:00 PM	Speaking Engagement	Speaking to law students on the importance of Dr. Martin Luther King, Jr.
7:30 PM	Dr. Martin Luther King, Jr. Dinner	A dinner honoring the dream of Dr. Martin Luther King, Jr.

While all of the events were important and exciting to me, I have to admit that my speaking engagement was incredibly meaningful. I was invited by the Michigan State University College of Law Black Law Students Association (BLSA). The Black Law Students Association is an organization formed to articulate and promote the needs and goals of black law students and effectuate change in the legal community. As I reflected on being the former Vice President of my alma mater's student organization, I was overjoyed to speak to an eager, hard-working student body.

I entered the law school's board room dressed somewhat conservatively with a gray suit, a white, crisp dress shirt, and a striped Burberry tie. I felt confident as I stood before the student body. The room was full of forty, energized and engaged law students. I knew that this was one of the perfect opportunities to give back. I had prepared a speech, which I started reading when I was introduced.

> "I am in awe of where I stand today. I sat where you sit, I have taken the courses you are taking, but there were times when I did not know, or even believe, that I was going to get here — to this place — this position in my life. Addressed now as State Representative Brian Banks of District One, I was once referred to as the defendant in the case of State of Michigan vs. Banks. Though widely known are my past and poor choices, little is known about what got me there and smaller still, what has gotten me here."

Somewhere into my speech I went off of my script and spoke about my personal experiences and my dream. I confessed to those students many of the offenses of my past. I told them about dropping out of high school, being on my own at twenty years old, getting anything and losing everything. I shared with them how hard I worked to let go of much of my past, but that there were three things I decided to hold on to.

The first thing was "vision". Somewhere along the way, when I was very young, I set a vision for myself that played like a movie screen in front of me over and over again. I remember seeing this movie play out while I was being sentenced in 1999. In the midst of the court proceedings, I began to think back on all of my goals and aspirations. It was important to me to get on the right path so I could make a better life for my family and the people I would serve.

Next, I conveyed to the students that I couldn't have made it this far without "hope", which I also held on to. My family, the judge and other people who believed in me told me that I could become anything I wanted to be and *that* gave me hope. They were the motivating forces in my life and fueled me every time I had to read one more precedent, take one more exam, or drive one more late night between Detroit and East Lansing.

Finally, I expressed to those students that I wouldn't have made it this far without "forgiveness". I needed to forgive myself and others who had hurt me, misguided me, and used me. I am my worse critic and you are probably your worse critic. Forgiving yourself is a challenging, daily, and necessary process. I have learned that ideas and good seeds that have been planted into my life could not grow in the negative, toxic ground of blame, guilt or self-defeat. I wanted to make sure they understood that life is going to happen. Sometimes things won't go as planned. Sometimes everything that can happen badly will happen. Sometimes you won't make the best decisions, but you cannot allow those things to breed negativity, guilt, or paralyzing shame.

As I closed my speech with those students, I couldn't help but to think, "It was all worth it. It had to happen." In fact, it had "2" happen; two things had to happen — the good things and the bad things. Without the good things, I couldn't have envisioned myself living a better life. Without the bad things, I wouldn't have learned who I really was and those things forced me to think about who I wanted to become.

There were some bad situations and I couldn't see any good emerging from them. Over time, it became clear to me that in every situation, good or bad, there is a lesson to be learned. The good things gave me hope and allowed me to see what was possible for me and the bad things showed me that I had a great amount of inner strength to endure, tenacity to keep going, and determination to never stop.

I continued on that evening to the dinner honoring Dr. King. At 34 years, 7 months, and 13 days of age, Dr. Martin Luther King, Jr. stood in front of the historical crowd on the steps of the Lincoln Monument and rendered the speech that would ring through the annals of time for ages to come. At 34 years, 11 months, and 22 days old, I'd won the seat for Michigan State Representative of District One. This moment was emotional for me as I pondered the importance of Dr. King's dream and reflected on the realization of my own. Two thirty-four-year-old, African American men, at two totally different times in history, who both aspired to uplift others and pushed for a dream. *How incredible is this?*

It's much easier to look back at a situation and say, "I should have" or "I could have" or "I would have". It's even easier to say what you would do if you were in someone else's shoes. However, when life happens to you, you don't expect it, therefore, you don't know how you will respond. I've learned that you need people in your life that can walk with you during the hard times. You can't make it through everything alone.

I also believe in God and I've had to learn how to trust Him through everything, even when it seems like a never-ending process. We live in a society that rushes to results, but the process to get to the end result is necessary; that's where we are developed. With God, you don't have to feel like you will never overcome failure. I had to learn that I would have moments of failure, but that failure does not mean defeat.

Failure is not permanent. Failure is simply an opportunity to learn a lesson to do better the next time. Some of the greatest people we know failed during their course of life, but ultimately became indisputable experts in their industries. When you don't achieve the goals that you want to achieve because of a terrible choice, don't beat up on yourself. Learn to adjust, forgive yourself (and forgive others), and move on to your ultimate goal. Take your time. A famous, English playwright, James Heywood, is known for saying, *"Rome wasn't built in a day, but they were laying bricks every hour."* Even if you've failed several times, you can always lay another brick.

I also realized that I could not compare myself, nor my journey, to anyone else's. Sometimes while we are on life's journey we happen to look at others and get distracted. Maybe you haven't gotten married yet or had children. Maybe you haven't completed your degree or purchased the house you want yet. Life happens. Please know that everyone's path will be different. Don't compare yourself to others because you don't know what they've had to endure to get to where they are. Truly, the grass is not always greener on the other side.

If I had known what I know now in the beginning, I would have told my 18-year-old self, "Take some time to refocus and reflect and don't try to rush through everything without learning some hard lessons." In fact, I would tell my 10-year-old self to remain a child a little longer and not rush getting older. I would tell my 20-year-old self to remain focused on my life goals and not allow anything nor anyone to get me off track to my goals. I would tell my 30-year-old self that, even with mistakes, I can still achieve goals. I would have encouraged myself to take one day at a time and not beat up on myself for my poor choices and decisions.

Unfortunately, my timing was a bit off from what was in my mind for my goals. The path I took deterred me from the "straight and narrow" one that I thought I should have taken. As I really began to look at myself, and what I had become, I started beating up on myself. I was extremely disappointed with myself. I was deeply wounded by my own self-inflicting, negative thoughts and words. I found myself upset and slipping into depression on more than one occasion.

The day after I resigned from public office was one of those occasions. I woke up with so many emotions. I was angry. I was hurt. I was disappointed. After all, I had worked so hard to obtain that seat again. I completed my Bachelor's, Master's, and Law degrees, and then ran for office three times. I could not believe what was happening. *What was happening to me?!*

I remember a friend telling me to take some time to think about all I had been through and, "Better yet, what are you going to do next?" she asked. I thought leaving office was going to be my demise, but boy was I mistaken. I had to do some self-reflection. I had to look at the glass as being half full and not half empty. I had to look for the lesson in what I had gone through and really own it and learn from it.

Once I came to grips with everything, and accepted things for what they were, I began to totally understand that, regardless to what happens in life, it's never too late to build again. If I hadn't learned this lesson, I wouldn't have started working for myself as a consultant. I never imagined that I would be working for myself, except for having my own law practice. I'm proud to say that my business has been doing quite well.

One thing I had to remember is: I'm human. I had to realize that there was going to be some mess ups along the way. I, like you, didn't always get it right, but, you and me, we have to continue working towards our goals while learning the lessons along the way. It wasn't easy and it won't be easy, but we can't give up on ourselves. Can we? No, we can't.

Before I laid my head down on my pillow that night, after the dinner honoring Dr. King, I had to take a moment and thank God for miraculously getting me through the criminal justice system. That system is not made to reform African Americans. It is made to further enslave our minds, our wills, and prevent the growth of our families.

Dr. Ashley Nellies reports in *The Color of Justice: Racial, Ethnic Disparity in State Prisons* that, "African Americans are incarcerated in state prisons across the country at more than five times the rate of whites, and at least ten times the rate in five states with many African Americans dying in prison and or not being rehabilitated." Dr. Nellies goes on to explain the alarming rate at which African Americans are caught up in the criminal justice system compared to their white counterparts.

When I dropped out of school, I felt like an unbelievably damaged boat in troubled water. Then there were days I felt like I didn't have a bridge over that water whatsoever either. I'm persuaded that God sustained me so I could be a leader in that system — so I can talk to fatherless young men, discouraged students, people who reverted to the streets, and constituents who are poor about how they can make it through anything regardless of past decisions and disappointments. They just need someone in their path who sees something worth saving in them, like people saw something worth saving in me.

On that day of celebration, I stood on the shoulders of Dr. King and others, who fought hard, with every inch of their being for their dreams. If I had known in the beginning – my beginning – that I could stand, on that National Holiday, as a college graduate, a law school graduate, and a State Representative, then I may have had fewer days being convinced that I didn't deserve it. So, I took my moment and I thanked God because I ended the day celebrating Dr. King's dream and mine.

Along with heroes like Dr. Martin Luther King, Congressman John Conyers Jr., Congressman John Lewis, Dean Connell Alsup, my grandfather, O.D., and many others, I possessed a foundation that is unbreakable; the foundation of God and church. I was taught to honor God in everything that I did. I learned principles of faith and trust at a young age. I realized that, but for the grace of God, I would not have been able to make it to where I am today.

It is because of God that I have my mere being. I know first-hand that faith can be a difficult concept for many people, whether you're just learning about God or you grew up attending weekly church services. Yes, it can be hard sometimes to believe in someone (without any doubt) that you can't see, touch, or hear. However, having a relationship with God requires believing beyond doubt and trusting in Him. Luckily, according to Christianity, faith is a gift from God, and not something you have to create on your own.

Now, doubt is real as well. Doubt is a natural human feeling so, if you're having trouble in believing in God, it does not necessarily mean you're doing anything wrong. Since you can't see God, it can be hard sometimes to trust that He's really there. However, if you check God's track record, you will see that He is there. Has there ever been a time when your back was against a wall and you didn't know how you were going to come out of a situation, but you did? I'm sure God stepped in for you like He did for me.

I have so much faith in God because I know personally that God has been there for me and has never failed me. When I went through the criminal justice system, it was only God that touched the heart of Judge Langford Morris to cause her to see something more in me than the charges I was facing. Circumstances where I was alone taught me to trust and depend on God. I've been in situations where everyone around me seemed to have disappeared. It seemed as if I was in a fight all alone. However, God always stepped in and came through for me. Even when I've felt worried and concern, all I had to do was look at God's track record in every area of my life and see that He had never failed me and I'm convinced that He won't fail now.

I also contribute overcoming numerous obstacles in my life to my support system, which is my community. My community consists of my family, close friends, classmates, colleagues, and even some of the constituents in the district where I served. It was these people that kept me rooted, grounded, and humble. You must have people in your corner. They should not only encourage, support, and pray for you, but also challenge you and tell you when you are wrong. It is very important to have voices in your ear that love you enough to disagree with you and still stick with you.

I am grateful that my community did not give up on me. They stayed in the fight with me and they were there for me in the most critical times. This isn't the end for me. I am ecstatic about the next chapter of my life. As a child I heard that "service is the price you pay for the space that you occupy." As long as I'm here on this earth I will be in service to others — helping the less fortunate, refusing to be judgmental, and paving the way for someone to come behind me. If I can persuade others to join me in service, we can all make our world a better place.

BIOGRAPHY

Honorable Brian R. Banks, M.Ed., J.D.

We all have dreams, but some of us never fully realize them. As seen with countless others who have faced extreme hardships, talent and tenacity are equally present in author, Brian Banks, who has realized many of his dreams. He is a law school graduate, educa- tor, community leader, and visionary. Born and raised in Detroit, Michigan, Brian shares the experiences with people who are underprivileged and disadvantaged. In spite of where he started, Brian always sensed that despite his small stature, he would take giant steps.

As a product of both a low-income and a single-parent family, Brian is personally and keenly aware of the difficult choices that today's youth face. He is intimately familiar with living in a home environment that was not full of love nor conducive for learning and growth. Brian saw a clear path — graduate from college, graduate from law school, become a prominent attorney, and then sit on the bench as an officer of the court. However, many things contributed to him taking a slightly different path.

In his book, *It Had 2 Happen: The Agony of Success,* Brian describes a defining moment of his life on a predestined day in 1999 when he stood before an Oakland County Circuit

Court judge who spoke life into him and acknowledged that she saw greatness on the inside of him that he did not even know still existed. This was Brian's "Revelation Day".

Brian currently holds both a Bachelor of Science in Criminal Justice and a Master of Education in Educational Leadership & Administration from Wayne State University. He has earned a Juris Doctor with a Concentration in Criminal Law from Michigan State University College of Law with his. Currently, Brian is pursuing a Ph.D. in Public Policy & Administration and has been an adjunct professor at Baker College.

On November 6, 2012, Mr. Banks was duly elected by the people of the 1st District to The Michigan House of Representatives, representing Northeast Detroit, Grosse Pointe Woods, Grosse Pointe Shores, and Harper Woods. Representative Banks served on several committees and was re-elected in 2014 and 2016. Throughout his terms, he was an advocate for education and committed to ensuring that all children have access to the quality education – no matter where they live. He continues his work to ensure Detroiters, and all urban and rural areas, get lower car insurance without compromising their benefits and protections.

Mr. Banks is a highly sought-after consultant, educator, organizer, assistant, community, political, legal mind and now, an author. Brian's work currently involves mentoring teens and young adults. He is called upon as a keynote speaker for Youth Day services at churches, college-bound student workshops, second chance programs, criminal justice reform seminars, and many more.